101 Select Sermon Outlines

101
SELECT SERMON
OUTLINES

by

Vaughan, Exell, Spurgeon, Robinson,
and Others

BAKER BOOK HOUSE
Grand Rapids 6, Michigan
1956

First Printing, October 1953
Second Printing, May 1956

Printed in the United States of Amercia

PREFACE

This is a compact volume of select sermon outlines from the sermon masters. Representative of those whose work is here made available are: Joseph S. Exell, Charles H. Spurgeon, F. B. Meyer, Charles J. Vaughan, Charles Simeon, Jabez Burns, and T. DeWitt Talmage. You will here find usable sermon outlines for every Sabbath of the year, as well as for such special occasions as: Church Dedication, Baccalaureate, New Year's Day, Good Friday, etc.

This is the sixth in the widely distributed and popular *Minister's Handbook Series*. It is preceded by: FUNERAL SERMONS AND OUTLINES, SERMONS AND OUTLINES ON THE LORD'S SUPPER, SERMONS AND OUTLINES FOR SPECIAL OCCASIONS, 1,001 SERMON ILLUSTRATIONS AND QUOTATIONS, and SERMONS AND OUTLINES ON THE SEVEN WORDS. In this series you will find a rich source of usable sermons, condensed sermons, meditations, extended outlines, brief outlines, suggested texts, sermon themes, pertinent illustrations, quotable poetry, and select hymns.

THE PUBLISHERS

1. The Creator and the Creation (Gen. 1:1)

I. THE WHOLE TRINITY, EACH IN HIS SEPARATE OFFICE, THOUGH ALL IN UNITY, ADDRESSED THEMSELVES TO THE WORK OF CREATION.

A. The Holy Spirit brooded over the watery chaos.

B. The Son, the Lord Jesus Christ, was the power, or "Arm of the Lord," by which the whole work was executed. "In the beginning was the Word."

C. The Father's mind willed all, planned all, and did all.

II. IF WE ASK WHY GOD CREATED THIS UNIVERSE OF OURS, THREE PURPOSES SUGGEST THEMSELVES.

A. It was the expression and outgoing of His wisdom, power, and love.

B. It was for the sake of His noblest work, His creature, man.

C. The heaven and earth were meant to be the scene of the exhibition of His own dear Son. Remember, that marvelously grand as it was, that first creation was only a type and earnest of a better. — J. VAUGHAN

2. The Creator and His Work (Gen. 1:1)

I. THEN ATHEISM IS A FOLLY. "In the beginning *God*."

A. Atheism is proved absurd by the history of the creation of the world. It would be impossible for a narrative to be clearer, more simple, or more divinely authenticated than that of creation. The very existence of things around us is indisputable evidence of its realty.

B. Atheism is proved absurd by the existence of the beautiful world around us. The world standing up around us in all its grandeur and design is a most emphatic assertion of the Being of God. Every flower is a denial of atheism. Every star is vocal with deity.

C. Atheism is proved absurd by the moral convictions of humanity. There is probably not an intelligent man in the wide universe, who does not believe in, and pay homage to, some deity or other.

7

II. Then Pantheism Is an Absurdity. "In the beginning *God created the heavens and the earth."*

We are informed by these verses that the world was a creation, and not a spontaneous, or natural emanation from a mysterious something only known in the vocabulary of a sceptical philosophy. Thus the world must have had a personal Creator, distinct and separate from itself.

III. Then Matter Is not Eternal. "In the *beginning."*

Thus it is evident that matter had a commencement. It was created by divine power. It had a birthday.

IV. Then the World Was Not the Result of a Fortuitous Combination of Atoms. "In the beginning God *created."*

Thus the world was a creation. There was the exercise of supreme intelligence. There was the expression in symbol of great thoughts, and also of divine sympathies.

V. Then Creation is the Outcome of Supernatural Power "In the beginning *God created."*

There must of necessity be much of mystery connected with this subject. Man was not present to witness the creation, and God has only given us a brief and dogmatic account of it. God is mystery. The world is a mystery. But there is far less mystery in the biblical account of the creation than in any other, as it is the most natural, the most likely — and also the most scientific, as it gives us an adequate cause for the effect. The re-creation of the soul is the explanation of the creation of the universe, and in fact of all the other mysteries of God.   — Joseph S. Exell

3. Enoch, or Walking with God (Gen. 5:24)

I. What Is Meant by Enoch's Walking with God?

A. That he was well-pleasing to God (Heb. 11:5). Amity, friendship, intimacy, love.

B. That he realized the divine presence (Heb. 11:6). God was to him a living Friend, in whom he confided, and by whom he was loved.

C. That he had very familiar intercourse with the Most High.

D. That this intercourse with God was continuous. He did not take a turn or two with God and then leave His company, but walked with God for hundreds of years. He did not commune with God by fits and starts, but abode in the conscious love of God.

E. That his life was progressive. At the end of two hundred years he was not where he began; he was not in the same company, but he had gone forward in the right way.

II. What Circumstances Were Connected with Enoch's Walking With God?

A. The details of his life are very few. It is quite enough for us to know that he walked with God.

B. It is a mistake to suppose that he was placed in very advantageous circumstances for piety.

1. He was a public man.

2. He was a family man.

3. He lived in a very evil age. Still he bore his witness for God.

III. What Was the Close of Enoch's Walk?

A. He finished his work early.

B. He was missed. "Not found" (Heb. 11:5).

C. His departure was a testimony.

— Charles H. Spurgeon

4. Tithes at the Start (Gen. 28:20-22)

The two important matters of notice, in this text, are the early purpose of this young patriarch to give a portion of his wealth to religious ends, and the establishment of a fixed system in presenting it. It seems to be in Scripture history the exact beginning of all that custom of tithing which meets us everywhere in the Old Testament. It has arrested my attention, because it is the act of a young man just starting in the new life. It furnishes me with this for a topic — *Systematic Beneficence: Its Principle and Its Measure.*

I. The Principle May Be Stated in One Compact Sentence: A Christian is to contribute, not on impulse, but by plan. Jacob seems to have understood in the outset that this was to be the practical side of his life.

A. This duty should be taken up early by every young Christian as a matter of study.

B. It will not do to discharge this work all at once. A settled habit of giving is promoted only by a settled exercise of giving.

C. It will not do to leave this duty to a mere impulse of excitement. Christians ought never to wait for fervid appeals or ardent addresses to sympathy.

D. It will not do to perform this duty as a mere mechanical form. We are told, in one familiar verse of the New Testament, that "he who soweth sparingly, shall reap also sparingly." This singular word "sparingly" occurs nowhere else in the Scriptures. It means grievingly, regretfully; holding back after the gift, if such an expression may be allowed.

E. This duty is to be discharged only with a diligent comparison of means with ends. System in giving is the secret of all success.

II.   The Measure of Christian Beneficence.

A. Give tithes to start with.

B. Tithes, just to start with, will in many cases force a Christian to increase as he progresses in material blessings. When life grows easier, and gains more plentiful, the good Lord, whose stewards we are, raises His rates of loan, and expects more liberal returns.

III.   Considerations which Enter into the Reckoning.

A. Think of what has been done in our behalf by God, our Maker and Redeemer. We should measure our gifts in money by our receipts in grace.

B. Remember whence the prosperity came, out of which we give money. God seeks where He has given.

C. Consider the extent of the work which is to be accomplished.

D. Think of the promises which reward the freegiver. "The liberal soul shall be made fat."

E. Think of the exigencies arising under the favoring providences of God.

F. Think of the listlessness of others.

Conclusion:

He that delays will harden. And it should never be forgotten

that money is only the measure of manhood when consecrated to Christ. It is ourselves we give to Him, ourselves He demands.
— CHARLES S. ROBINSON

5. The New Date (or, A Sermon for the New Year)
(Exod. 12:2)

We have here a new event, a new starting point — a new epoch, and therefore, a new era. That event was emancipation, a redemption, an exodus. There were centuries behind of exile and servitude; of that experience which has been so characteristic of Israel, a sojourning which was no naturalization, a dwelling *among,* without becoming *of,* another nation; estrangement, therefore isolation, solitude, even in populous cities, and amidst teeming multitudes. Now, all this is behind them. They are to quit the homeless home. Egypt behind, Sinai before, Canaan beyond, this is the exact account of the position of Israel when the words of the text were spoken. Redemption was the starting point of the new; from it all that follows shall take a new character, and a new life.

I. THE IDEA OF A NEW START IS NATURALLY ATTRACTIVE TO ALL OF US. We are fatigued, we are wearied, we are dissatisfied, and justly so, with the time past of our lives. We long for a gift of amnesty and oblivion.

II. THERE ARE SENSES IN WHICH THIS IS IMPOSSIBLE. The continuity of life cannot be broken. There is a continuity, a unity, an identity, which annihilation could only destroy.

III. "THE BEGINNING OF MONTHS" IS MADE BY AN EXODUS. Redemption is the groundwork of the new life. If there is in any of us a real desire for change, we must plant our feet firmly on Redemption.

IV. WHEN WE GET OUT OF EGYPT WE MUST REMEMBER THAT THERE IS STILL SINAI IN FRONT, with its thunderings and voices. We have to be schooled and disciplined by processes not joyous but grievous. These processes cannot be hurried, they must take their time. Here we must expect everything that is changeful, and unresting, and unreposeful, within as without. But he who has promised will perform. He who has redeemed will save. He who took charge will also bring through. — CHARLES J. VAUGHAN

6. Help to Temperance (Lev. 10:9-11)

(Combine with this verse Jer. 35:6; Eph. 5:18; I Thess. 5:7.)

Intemperance is one of the major evils of our land, self-imposed. This is its saddest feature. All the evils connected with it might be swept away if men so willed. There are various paths towards the removal of the evil of intemperance.

I. THE NATURAL. Use no intoxicants; and thus never acquire a passion for them.

II. THE MEDICAL. Some treat drunkedness as a disease; and by medicine seek to destroy the appetite for alcohol.

III. THE SANITARY. Asylums for inebriates have been opened, which combine physical and moral means to effect a cure; and with a measure of success.

IV. THE LEGAL. Its object is to control or arrest the evil; and by prohibition of its manufacture and sale, to remove it from the land.

V. THE VOLUNTARY. This involves the pledge and membership in societies banded together for mutual help and safety (A. A.). Earnest work for others is a good preventative, so long as it is actively continued.

VI. THE PHILANTHROPIC. Here is a reform in which to engage. This seeks to produce a change in sentiment through education and enlightenment as to the evil results of intemperance.

VII. THE SPIRITUAL. Grace, wherever received, casts out the demon of drink. The only real cure.

— LEWIS O. THOMPSON (Adapted)

7. The Jubilee; or, The Degenerative and Corrective Force of Society (Lev. 25:13)

INTRODUCTION:
1. The degenerative forces of society are in itself.
2. The corrective forces of society are from God.

I. MAN IS SUPERIOR TO PROPERTY. By dissolving the relation between creditor and debtor, master and slave, God declared that the debtor was more valuable than the debt, the slave more valuable than the secular claims of his master. The poorest laborer in your employ is greater than all your capital, the poorest renter than all your real estate. The violation of this truth is the ruin of society, and it is violated every day. Man, in our society, is held cheap in comparison with property and wealth. That is our curse.

II. GOD IS THE DISPOSER OF PROPERTY. His putting an end to the claims of the creditor, employer, and landowner, indicates this. "The earth is the Lord's and the fullness thereof."

III. SOCIETY HAS HIGHER WANTS THAN PROPERTY. In the year of jubilee labor was checked, and a period given for spiritual services. Let us control and modify our labor in the interest of spiritual exercises, our love for wealth in the interest of love for our neighbor, and our evaluation of earthly gain in the interest of treasures in heaven.   — DAVID THOMAS (Adapted)

8. Balaam Obstruced by the Angel (Num. 22:31)

I. GOD OFTEN MERCIFULLY INTERPOSES TO OBSTRUCT SINNERS IN THEIR WAYS.

II. HIS MOST SIGNAL INTERPOSITIONS OFTEN EXCITE ONLY THE WRATH OF THOSE FOR WHOSE BENEFIT THEY ARE SENT.

III. THOSE INTERPOSITIONS WHICH ARE ACKNOWLEDGED TO HAVE BEEN SENT IN MERCY, PRODUCE, FOR THE MOST PART, A VERY TRANSIENT EFFECT.   — CHARLES SIMEON

9. The Paternal Character of God (Deut. 32:6)

I. GOD AS THE FATHER OF HIS PEOPLE.
A. God is the Author of their spiritual existence.
B. He makes paternal provision for His children.
C. He affords paternal protection to His children.
D. He imparts paternal instruction.
E. He takes paternal delight in His children.
F. He administers paternal correction to His children.
G. He lays up a paternal provision for His children.

II. The Claims Which He Has upon His Children.

A. He ought to receive from us the highest reverence. We should cultivate His fear.

B. He ought to have our supreme affections. "Thou shalt love the Lord thy God . . . ."

C. He should possess our unwavering confidence. Trust in Him at all times.

D. He should have our cheerful obedience. "Be ye followers of God as dear children . . . ."

E. He shall receive from us our most exalted praises.

— Jabez Burns

10. The Pile of Stones Speaking (Josh. 4:1-24)

It is entirely improper to build a house like this, occupying so much space, and with such expenditure of labor and outlay of money, unless there be some very good reasons for doing it; and so I demand of all who have assisted in the building of this structure: "What mean ye by these stones?"

I. We Mean That They Shall Be an Earthly Residence for Christ. Jesus did not have much of a home when He was here. Oh, Jesus! is it not time that Thou hadst a house? We give Thee this. Thou didst give it to us first, but we give it back to Thee. It is too good for us, but not half good enough for Thee.

II. We Mean the Communion of Saints.

III. We Mean by These Stones the Salvation of the People. We did not build this church for mere worldly reforms, or for an educational institution, or as a platform on which to read essays and philosophical discourses; but a place for the tremendous work of soul-saving. Do not make the blunder of the ship carpenters in Noah's time, who helped to build the ark, but did not get into it.   — T. DeWitt Talmage

11. Faint, Yet Pursuing (Judg. 8:4)

Let us, then, notice respecting Gideon,

I. His Ready Obedience to the Divine Call.

A. When convinced that God had called him to fight for Israel, he delayed not to execute his commission.

C. The language of the prophets. What does Jeremiah say concerning his own writings? The Lord commanded Jeremiah to set
down in a book certain prophecies. Those prophecies Baruch read
in the audience of the king and the princes. And what is said
respecting Baruch's reading? "Then read he in the book the words
of the Lord in the house of the Lord." He read in the book "the
words of the Lord."

D. The language of Christ. He met His adversaries with the
Scripture.

E. The language of the Evangelists and Apostles. Our Lord,
before His departure, promised to send to His disciples the Holy
Ghost. "And when He is come, He will bring all things to your
remembrance whatsoever I have spoken unto you." The Evangelists and Apostles, therefore, wrote under the controlling power
of the Holy Ghost. "All Scripture," wrote St. Peter, "is given by
inspiration of God," or, is "God-breathed." That Scripture Timothy had known from a child; and that Scripture was able to make
Timothy "wise unto salvation through faith in Christ Jesus." By
that term "Scripture," which was able to make its readers savingly
acquainted with Christ, was meant the Old Testament writings.
Now, these Old Testament books are directly quoted or alluded to
in the New Testament several hundreds of times. There are more
than eighty such references in St. Matthew; more than thirty in
St. Mark; more than fifty in St. Luke; forty in St. John; more
than fifty in the Acts of the Apostles; more than seventy in the
Romans.

II. Words of Counsel.

A. Beware of the sin of unbelief. God has given us a revelation.
"The mighty God, even the Lord, hath spoken." That revelation
contains difficulties and mysteries. Our Lord was satisfied with
the Old Testament, and we, therefore, should be satisfied. But
we have, in addition, a most clear commentary on the Old Testament. We have the New Testament.

B. Cultivate a childlike spirit. Our Lord has plainly told us
that, except we be converted and become as little children, we
shall not enter the kingdom of heaven.

C. Receive all that the Bible reveals. In the Bible, as St. Peter
tells us, there are many things "hard to be understood." This is no
more than we ought to expect, when the infinite God reveals Himself to a finite being like man. Those things, however, which are
necessary for our salvation — sin, death, hell, heaven, and general

resurrection, the atonement of Christ, the work of the Spirit —
are written so plainly "that he may run that reads."

— C. CLAYTON

15. Ahab's Sin and Repentance (I Kings 21:27)

There is much in this old chronicle of sin and doom which we
may ponder with profit. Let me try to bring out of it some present-
day lessons of warning and admonition.

I. HAPPINESS CONSISTS, NOT IN HAVING, BUT IN BEING.
How many even today are letting their lives be darkened because
some Naboth denies them a vineyard, or some Mordecai will not
salute them! They forget that even if they had the things which
they so long for, happiness would be as far from them as ever,
and some new object would take the place of their old grievance.
They do lack one thing. But that one thing is not external to them,
but within them. They lack a new heart; and until they get that
they can have no abiding satisfaction. "Whosoever drinketh of this
water shall thirst again."

II. THE EVIL OF UNHALLOWED ALLIANCES. Dazzled with the
glitter of a fortune, or the glare of a high position, a young person
enters into the sacred alliance of matrimony with one who has no
moral stability or Christian excellence, and the issue is certain
misery, with the probable addition of crime and disaster.

III. THE PERVERSION WHICH AN EVIL HEART MAKES OF
RELIGIOUS KNOWLEDGE. There is a Spanish proverb somewhat to
this effect, "When the serpent straightens himself, it is that he
may go into his hole." So when the unscrupulous suddenly manifest some scrupulous regard for legal forms or for religious ob-
servances, you may be sure that they are after mischief. Some of
the blackest crimes that have ever been committed have been
perpetrated through the forms of law, or under the color of
religion. Is it not true that "the heart is deceitful above all things,
and desperately wicked"? and we are forcibly impressed with the
fact that no one is so daringly defiant in wickedness as he who
knows the truth and disregards it? Mere knowledge never yet saved
any one from ruin; for, if the heart be perverted, everything that
enters the head is only made subservient to its iniquity. Your
educated villains are all the more dangerous because of their educa-

tion; and among godless men they are the most to be dreaded who have an intelligent acqaintance with the Word of God.

IV. THE PRICE WHICH WE HAVE TO PAY FOR SIN. What weighty words are these of Elijah to Ahab, "Thou hast sold thyself to work evil in the sight of the Lord!" The great German poet has elaborated this thought into that weird production in which he represents his hero as selling his soul to the mocking Mephistopheles. And it were well that every evil-doer took to heart the moral of his tragic tales. That which the sinner gives for his unhallowed pleasure or dishonest gain is himself. Consider it well.

V. THE CURSE WHICH ATTENDS ILL-GOTTEN GAINS. The gains of ungodliness are weighted with the curse of God; and, sooner or later, that will be made apparent. For the moral government of God today is administered on the same principles as those which we find underlying this narrative. True, the dishonest man now pursuing his purposes in secret may have no Elijah sent to him, with the special mission to declare to him the sort of punishment which shall overtake him; but Elijah's God is living yet, and one has only to open his eyes, and mark the progress of events from year to year, to be convinced that "sorrow tracketh wrong, as echo follows song — on, on, on."

VI. THE TENDERNESS OF GOD TOWARD THE PENITENT. Ahab was filled with bitter regret at what had been done, and God, who will not break the bruised reed or quench the smoking flax, said that the evil should not come in his day. If God were so considerate of Ahab, the idolater, the murderer, the thief, will He not regard thee, O thou tearful one! who are bemoaning the number and aggravation of thy sins? Go then, to Him; and let this be thine encouragement.   — WILLIAM M. TAYLOR

16. Gehazi (II Kings 5:20-27)

Let us derive a few general and useful reflections from the whole narrative.

I. PERSONS MAY BE VERY WICKED UNDER RELIGIOUS ADVANTAGES. The means of grace and the grace of the means are very distinguishable from each other, and are frequently found separate.

II. Here Is a Warning against the Love of Money. "Take heed, and beware of covetousness."

III. See the Encroachments and Progress of Sin; and learn how dangerous it is to give way to any evil propensity.

IV. How Absurd It Is to Sin With an Expectation of Secrecy! "There is no darkness nor shadow of death where the workers of iniquity can hide themselves."

V. Abhor and Forsake Lying. It is in most cases peculiarly easy to detect falsehood. Hence it is said that every liar should have a good memory. And what an odious character is a liar! How shunned and detested when discovered! To every mortal upon earth, the appellation of a liar is the most detestable. A liar is the emblem of "the devil, who was a liar from the beginning, and abode not in the truth."

Remember Gehazi!   — William Jay

17. The Prayer of Jabez (I Chron. 4:9, 10)

We will without any formal divisions simply endeavor to travel through the petitions offered up in this prayer of Jabez.

I. First Petition: "Oh, that thou wouldest bless me."

A. There are many apparent blessings which may prove real curses.

1. Health. Its tendency is to remove far away all thoughts of death and eternity; to make a man more or less satisfied with the things of the present; and to draw comfort from the creature instead of the Creator.

2. Money. It often shuts up the heart, results in pride, and becomes a temptation and a snare.

3. The good opinion and praise of men.

B. There are apparent curses which often are real blessings.

1. Ill health.

2. Poverty.

3. The criticism of fellow men.

C. There are blessings which are both apparent and real.

1. The fear of the Lord.

2. Intimation of God's favor.

3. The revelation of Christ to the soul.

4. Unreserved trust in God.

5. An appetite after God's Word.

II. SECOND PETITION: "And enlarge my coast." A coast means a boundary line, such as divides one territory from another, or terminates a country, as the sea-coast is the boundary of an island. Every quickened soul has a coast — the territory of inward experience — which is limited and bounded by the line that the Holy Spirit has drawn in his conscience.

A. Some have a narrow experience; they cannot get beyond doubts and fears, guilt and convictions, with at times earnest desires for mercy and pardon.

B. Others have their coast a little more extended. They are enabled to hope in God's mercy, and anchor in His promises.

C. Others can through faith rest in Christ's blood and righteousness, having received some intimation of favor, but not brought into the full liberty of the gospel.

D. Others are brought into the life, light, liberty, joy and peace of the gospel. The living soul cannot but earnestly desire to have his coast enlarged. More light, more life, more liberty, more feeling, more knowledge of God in Christ, more faith, hope, and love. To have his heart enlarged in prayer, meditation, communion, and in affection to the people of God.

III. THIRD PETITION: "And that Thy hand might be with me." A living child wants to see and feel a fatherly hand with him and over him, going before him, holding him up spiritually, clearing his path, and giving him testimonies that what is done in his fear shall terminate in his approbation. So also the child of God.

IV. FOURTH PETITION: "And that Thou wouldest keep me from evil." Every child of God will be more or less frequently offering up this prayer. Shun evil, and shun anyone who makes light of sin. Evil is a grief, a burden to every living soul.

— J. C. PHILPOT

18. Jehoshaphat's Connection with Ahab Reproved
(II Chron. 19:2)

I. What Is That Intimacy with the Ungodly Which God Forbids.

A. An alliance with them.

B. A conformity to them.

C. An unnecessary association with them.

II. Why It Is so Displeasing to Him.

A. On account of the state of mind it implies.

B. On account of its pernicious tendency.

C. On account of its opposition to his revealed will.

— Charles Simeon

19. Dedicating the Temple (Ezra 6:14-22)

We are here advised as to the accessories by which the builders of the temple were enabled to succeed.

I. God Was with Them. All along He had been predisposed in their behalf. We also are exhorted to work out our own salvation because it is God that worketh in us both to will and to do.

II. God Was Pleased to Communicate with Them Through His Ordained Servants. Haggai was an old man whose strength lay largely in admonition. Zechariah was younger, more inclined to the dreaming of hopeful dreams and the seeing of bright visions.

III. They Were Encouraged by the Favorable Attitude of Temporal Princes. The dedication took place in the month Adar, "the month of splendor," so called because of the brightness of its suns and the beauty of its flowers.

A. A hundred bullocks, two hundred rams, and four hundred lambs were offered in sacrifice; "and for a sin offering, twelve he goats for all Israel." There is something pathetic in the mention of these he goats. Ten of the twelve tribes, having cut themselves loose from their brethren, had little or no part in the building of this temple, but they were remembered, and a place in the sin offering was sacredly reserved for them. It was as when mothers set vacant chairs for their absent, wayward sons on Thanksgiving Day. Whatever might happen, the religious unity of Israel must be preserved. In like manner the Church of Christ, however parted asunder by the controversies of the past, should be as one in the work of the kingdom and in the rejoicings of the triumph of Christ.

B. At this dedication the ancient order of service was restored. The assignments of the priests and Levites date back to the time of Moses (Num. 2:6-10). It does not follow that because a custom is old it is obsolete. Prayer is as old as human want, like the air we breathe, and time can make no improvement upon it. It should be observed that the Feast of Passover was among the venerable customs which were revived at this dedication. It was a foreshadowing of the atonement of Christ, without which all other pomp and circumstance of service are a dumb show.

— DAVID J. BURRELL

20. A God Ready to Pardon (Neh. 9:17)

I. THE HISTORY OF ISRAEL SINGULARLY ILLUSTRATES THE READINESS OF GOD TO PARDON.

II. IT IS EQUALLY TRUE THAT THE LORD AT ALL TIMES IS A GOD READY TO PARDON.

A. It is true of Him by nature. Mercy is an essential attribute of God.

B. He Himself removed the impediment which lay in the way of forgiveness.

C. He sends His message of love to sinners while they are yet in their sins.

D. He makes no hard conditions with sinners.

E. What He demands of man by the gospel He also works in Him by His Spirit.

F. He accepts even the very lowest grade of the necessary graces. Repentance, etc.   — CHARLES H. SPURGEON

21. Attachment to God's House (Neh. 11:16)

I. THE RESOLUTION ITSELF: "We will not forsake . . ." This resolution includes —

A. Constant and regular attendance.

B. A lively interest in its welfare and prosperity.

II. THE GROUNDS OF THIS RESOLUTION.

A. Our gracious union with God. All connected with God should be dear and sacred to us — His Word, ordinances, people; therefore His house.

B. Our clear and imperative duty. Public worship is of God's appointment.

C. Our public profession.

D. The special advantages derived from it. Exaltation of desires; soul elevation; enlargement of mind; soul enrichment with all spiritual blessings in Christ. "A day in Thy courts is better than a thousand . . . ." "They that wait upon the Lord . . . ."

E. The connection of the house of God with the celestial world. It is "the gate of heaven."

III. APPLICATION.

A. Where professors are indifferent to the welfare of God's house, it is an unfailing indication that the heart is not right with God.

B. Let the subject inspire the sincere friends of Christ to more ardent zeal for the diffusion of the Divine glory.

C. How suited is God's house to every description. The reckless here are warned, the supine aroused, the inquirer directed, the mourner comforted, the faithful established, etc. — JABEZ BURNS

22. Providence — As Seen in the Book of Esther
(Esth. 11:1)

From the narrative of the preceding chapters we learn that —

I. GOD PLACES HIS AGENTS IN FITTING PLACES FOR DOING HIS WORK.

II. THE LORD NOT ONLY ARRANGES HIS SERVANTS, BUT HE RESTRAINS HIS ENEMIES.

III. GOD IN HIS PROVIDENCE TRIES HIS PEOPLE.

IV. THE LORD'S WISDOM IS SEEN IN ARRANGING THE SMALLEST EVENTS SO AS TO PRODUCE GREAT RESULTS.

V. THE LORD IN HIS PROVIDENCE CALLS HIS OWN TO BE ACTIVE.

VI. IN THE END THE LORD ACHIEVES THE TOTAL DEFEAT OF HIS FOES AND THE SAFETY OF HIS PEOPLE.

Lessons:

1. It is clear that the divine will is accomplished, and yet men are perfectly free agents.

2. What wonders can be wrought without miracles! In the miracles of Pharaoh we see the finger of God, but in the wonders of providence, without miracle, we see the hand of God.

3. How safe the Church of God is!

4. The wicked will surely come to an ill end.

5. Let each child of God rejoice that we have a Guardian so near the throne. Every Jew in Shushan must have felt hope when he remembered that the queen was a Jewess. Today, let us be glad that Jesus is exalted.   — CHARLES H. SPURGEON

23. On Justification (Job 25:4)

I. WHAT JUSTIFICATION IS. The being accounted righteous though we are not so. When brought into a justified state we are treated as if we were altogether righteous. Whose is this righteousness? Whence is it derived? Not from ourselves or any excellence in human nature. We must be accounted righteous, and justified with God, by other merits than our own. It is to the grace of our Lord Jesus Christ that we are indebted.

II. HOW A MAN CANNOT BE JUSTIFIED.

A. Not by repentance.

B. Not by amendment of life.

C. Not by our sincerity.

D. Not by any works whatever of our own.

III. HOW ALONE HE CAN BE JUSTIFIED. We are accounted righteous before God only for the merit of our Lord and Saviour Jesus Christ by faith, and not for our own works or deservings. Why does faith alone, faith without works, justify us? Because faith is the only medium by which we can receive Christ.

IV. Why a Man Can Be Justified in No Other Way Than the Way in Which He Is Justified.

A. It is God's determination that "no flesh shall glory in His sight."

B. God has determined that His Son alone shall be exalted in the justification of a sinner.

C. It is God's determination to magnify His name and word above all the philosophy and traditions of men.

D. It is a merciful God's gracious determination to afford grounds of the most abundant consolation to the humbled and believing sinner.   — W. Mudge

24. The Glory of God (Ps. 19:1)

Nature exists not for a merely natural, but for a moral end; not for what it is, but for what it says or declares.

I. What Nature Tells Us to Think of God.

A. Nature reveals God. The race as a whole have heard the declaration of His eternal power and Godhead. In proportion as they have heard, adoring, they have risen in the scale of manhood.

B. Nature declares the knowledge and power of God. The marks of mathematical and geometric law in nature are conspicuous. The more we explore the different departments of nature, the more we find it pervaded by strict arithmetical and dynamic laws. We meet "thought" everywhere. The race of man, as a whole, has heard, and to some extent understood, the testimony of nature to infinite thought and power.

C. Nature declares that God is just and good. This has been called in question. Nature says that every natural law, if obeyed, tends to happiness. Nature's laws are benevolent. Men have not fully appreciated this, for one reason, because they have so commonly broken those laws and have suffered. But does nature in any wise speak of the divine mercy? This question has often been wrongly answered. Listen attentively, and you will hear nature say that God is merciful. It is a striking fact that very many, if not all, physical penalties can be mitigated, if not relieved, by some counter law, some curious side-process or arrangement. God has so made nature as practically to encourage self-sacrifice for each other. Whenever men take pains for each other, to help each other over their faults and their consequences, there is an illustration, however faint, of the divine principle of mercy. Mercy is the policy of the divine government; it is the character of God himself.

II. What God Thinks of Nature.

A. God looks upon nature as a basis of language. Let the heavenly orbs be for signs. Signs are vehicles of ideas. Let them say something; let them be words. The universe is God's telephone, God's grand signal service system by which He can flash messages from the heights above to the deepest valleys below. The material system is God's great instrument of conversation.

B. God tells us what to think of his eloquent material system. It is God's most glorious schoolroom by which to teach us reality, — above all, to teach us self-government, and painstaking for one another. Why are we in such a world? Because we needed to be. We need what we get here. We need that knowledge of ourselves which nature can give. We need to be where we are. We need just the restraints and the liberties, the trials and the triumphs, the joys and the sorrows, the smiles and the tears, the bliss and the anguish of this strange life. And in all, and through all, we need to know Him who placed us here, and is revealing Himself to us in a thousand ways.   — Charles Beecher

25. The Religious Faculty (Ps. 42:2)

I. Its Reality. "My soul thirsteth for God." Do human beings desire God in that intense way? We are all acquainted with some physical sensations of that intensity. We have all felt thirst, or at least we can imagine thirst, which is almost delirious in its desire for water. But is there anything in the human mind in connection with God that is as intense as that? I dare say most of us have had feelings to some fellow-creature that this would hardly be too strong to describe. The absence or the loss of somebody has made us sick with desire, almost sick unto death, whereas the return or the presence of the same person has made us indescribably happy. But are there any feelings in the human heart towards God comparable to these? Is there in human nature a thirst for God to be compared with the thirst for knowledge or the thirst for beauty? Open a book like St. Augustine's "Confessions," or "The Imitation of Christ," and on every page you will find it.

II. ITS UNIVERSALITY. Wherever men are found they are religious beings. Religion is an element of human life everywhere, and everywhere it is an ideal and a refining element. In fact it is now generally acknowledged that the blossom and flower of every civilization is its religion, and even the most sceptical of men will now sometimes allow that the rational satisfaction of man's religious nature is, and always will be, the greatest desideratum of the human race.

III. ITS MANIFESTATIONS.

A. It is often an intellectual thirst, a thirst for an explanation of the tangle and mystery of existence. You have a classical illustration of that in the Book of Job, where the hero, blinded with the whirl and confusion of things, cries out for a sight of Him who rides upon the storm.

B. Still oftener, perhaps, the thirst for God is a thirst of the heart. All men, especially all women, know in some degree what it is to wish to be loved, to be thought about and cared for. These sentiments, as a rule, find their satisfaction in the domestic affections, and sometimes these are so satisfying as to fill up the whole desire. But this satisfaction is not conceded to all; and from some who have had it, it is taken away; and I rather think that all sometimes feel that they require love larger, more sympathetic, more intelligent and enduring than any human love. In fact it is only the love of God that can thoroughly satisfy the heart.

C. The thirst for God is still oftener, and more conspicuously, a thirst of the conscience. The conscience, although generally a very quiet element in our nature, may become a very clamorous one. It cries out for deliverance from guilt. It cries out for deliverance from temptation and sin. And the reason why Christianity has been such a consolation to mankind is because it has so thoroughly answered. "The blood of Jesus Christ, God's Son, cleanseth us from all sin." Under the lashes of conscience, man cries out, "O wretched man that I am, who shall deliver me from the body of this death?" But Christianity answers, "Thanks be to God, through Jesus Christ our Lord."

IV. ITS CULTURE. The religious faculty requires constant exercise, if there is to be any comprehensiveness and certainty of religious experience. Are you cultivating your religious faculty, or are you neglecting it, and allowing it to atrophy?

A. The first thing that is needed for the culture of the religious faculty is the careful observance of the Sabbath. The cessation from toil, the preaching of the gospel, the atmosphere of peace, the influence of united worship, tend to call the religious nature out, encouraging it to revel in its native element.

B. The other opportunity for this kind of culture is prayer. That brings the religious nature nearer to its object than anything else. I remember, when a boy, hearing some one say, "backsliding always begins at the closet door." — JAMES STALKER

26. The Twofold Song of the Believer (Ps. 101:1)

I. MERCY.

A. What is it? Goodness and kindness to the undeserving.

B. What is there in mercy, of which we ought to sing?

1. The marvelousness of its origin.

2. The expensiveness of its sacrifices.

3. The abundance of its blessings.

4. Its universality and freeness.

5. As to other special distinctions of mercy. Its length — from eternity to eternity. Its height — higher than the heavens, and above the clouds. Its perpetuity — it endureth for ever. Besides, it is said to be strong, rich, tender, faithful; and above all, God Himself delighteth in it. What a theme then for holy contemplation and joyous song!

II. JUDGMENT. This may mean —

A. God's righteousness.

B. God's law.

C. God's wrath.

D. God's chastening dispensations.

1. Their wise administration.

2. The tenderness of their application.

3. The support He gives with them.

4. The great ends His judgments are to accomplish.

Conclusion:

1. Have we not a keynote which ought to suit every heart and voice?

2. The advantages of this joyous course will be many. It will lighten the load of sorrow. It will sweeten the bitter potion. It

will while away the dreary hour. It will exhilarate the oppressed and fainting heart. It will, by a kind of divine chemistry, bring new elements of health and comfort out of nauseous medicines. It will cheer the soul, honor religion, glorify your Father, and aid greatly in your spiritual and upward flight to the land of eternal joy and everlasting glory.

3. May some now learn to sing the Lord's song in a strange land.

4. Sing on the way to heaven, in the expectation of singing there, for ever and ever.   — JABEZ BURNS

27. The First Rudiments of Knowledge (Prov. 1:7)

The fear of the Lord is an abiding and reverent sense of the presence of God and of accountableness to Him. For this to exist God must be that real, personal Being which we have every reason to believe God has revealed Himself to be: such in character, as to love holiness, and justice, as He has declared Himself in His Word.

WHY IS THIS FEAR THE BEGINNING OF KNOWLEDGE?

A. Because knowledge being the apprehension of facts, and application of them to life, it cannot properly begin, or be based on a right foundation, without first apprehending and applying a fact which includes and which modifies all other facts whatever.

B. Because knowledge is the food of the soul. And what is the soul? What ought its stores and its accumulated powers to be, and to be useful for? The knowledge which is to feed and train the soul must begin, continue, and end, in the apprehension of Him.

C. Because knowledge, as the mere accumulation of facts, is inoperative upon life. If you would be worth anything to society, worth anything to your own families, worth anything to yourselves, the fear of God must come first in your thoughts and lives. The fear of God is the first thing; the consciousness of Him about you, the laying down His revealed facts respecting Himself and you as your greatest facts; the setting up of His will as the inner law of your being.   — HENRY ALFORD

28. Keeping Company With Fools (Prov. 13:20)

"But a companion of fools shall be destroyed."

I. Who Are Fools?

A. Those who occupy their time and thought with trifles.

B. Those who "make a mock at sin."

C. Those who neglect important truths and realities.

D. Those who do not prepare for great and unavoidable events.

II. How Do We Walk with Them?

A. By frequenting their company.

B. By following their examples.

C. By reading their books.

III. What Will Be the Consequences?

A. We will be tainted with their vices.

B. We shall share their present sufferings.

C. We shall be involved in their eternal doom.

— W. W. Wythe

29. Remembering God in Our Youth (Eccl. 12:1)

I. What Is Implied in "Remembering Our Creator."

A. His authority over us.

B. The commands he has given us.

C. His continual presence with us.

D. His determination to judge us in the last day.

II. Why We Should Thus Remember Him in Early Life. It were easy to accumulate reasons on so plain a point: but we shall content ourselves with assigning a few of the most obvious,

A. This is the most favorable time.

B. It may be for aught we know, the only time that shall be allotted us.

C. No other thing in the universe can so contribute to our present happiness.

D. There will certainly come a time when we shall wish we had sought the Lord in early life.

— Charles Simeon

30. Christ and the Believer (Song of Sol. 2:2)

I. What Christ Thinks of the Believer. "As the lily among thorns, so is my love among the daughters."

A. See what Christ thinks of the unconverted world. It is like a field full of briars and thorns in His eyes.

1. Because fruitless.

2. Because, when the Word is preached among them, it is like sowing among thorns.

3. Because their end will be like that of thorns — they are dry and fit only for the burning.

B. See what Christ thinks of the Believer. "As the lily among thorns, so is my love among the daughters."

1. Because justified in the eyes of Christ; washed in His blood, he is pure and white as a lily.

2. A believer's nature is changed. Once he was like the barren, prickly thorn, fit only for burning. Now Christ has put a new spirit in him. The dew has been given to him, and he grows up like the lily.

3. The believer is lonely in the world. Observe, there is but one lily, but many thorns. There is a great wilderness all full of thorns, and only one lonely flower. So there is a world lying in wickedness, and a little flock that believes in Jesus.

II. What the Believer Thinks of Christ. "As the apple tree among the trees of the wood."

A. Christ is most precious in the eye of the believer. As a weary and hungry traveller would prefer an apple tree to any other kind, because he would find both shelter and nourishing food under it, so the believer prefers Christ above all. Oh! there is no rest for the soul except under that branch which God has made strong. My heart's desire and prayer for you is, that you may all find rest there.

B. Why has the believer so high an esteem of Christ?

1. Because he has made trial of Christ.

2. Because he sat down with great delight.

— Robert M. McCheyne

31. Isaiah's Sermon (Isa. 1:2-31)

The sermon which is contained in this chapter has in it —

I. A High Charge Exhibited in God's Name against the Jewish Church and Nation.

A. For their ingratitude (vv. 2, 3).

B. For their incorrigibleness (v. 5).

C. For the universal corruption and degeneracy of the people (vv. 4, 6, 21, 22).

D. For their rulers' perverting of justice (v. 23).

II. A Sad Complaint of the Judgments of God which they had brought upon themselves by their sins, and by which they were brought almost to utter ruin (vv. 7-9).

III. A Just Rejection of the Shows and Shadows of Religion which they kept up among them, notwithstanding this general defection and apostasy (vv. 10-15).

IV. An Earnest Call to Repentance and Reformation, setting before them life and death (vv. 16-20).

V. A Threatening of Ruin to Those That Would Not Be Reformed (vv. 24, 28-31).

VI. A Promise of a Happy Reformation at Last, and a return to their primitive purity and prosperity (vv. 25-27). And all this is to be applied by us, not only to the communities we are members of, in their public interests, but to the state of our own souls.   — Matthew Henry

32. Christian Joy (Isa. 9:3)

I. The Fact of Their Joy. "They joy." Who? Those who, embracing the light of the Gospel, and renouncing the hidden works of darkness, are made the children of the light and of the day.

A. It is divine in its nature. The joy of the men of the world, however diversified it may be, has its spring and source in the world. The joy of the ambitious has its rise in the pride of the world. The joy of the miser has its spring in the riches of the world. The joy of the sensualist is derived from the pleasures of the world. But believers are taught better.

B. It is extensive in its grounds. God — their Christian privileges — their Christian prospects.

C. It is salutary in its effects. Its tendency is good.

II. The Peculiarity of Their Joy. "Before Thee." This is an expressive term and intimates several things.

A. It is spiritual. It is a joyful state of mind, connected with that Divine Being who is a Spirit. Every exercise of the mind that unites us to Him must be spiritual.

B. It is sincere. The Christian's joy is real, not imaginary. It will bear inspection.

C. It is secret. As the world knows not the extent of our sorrows, so it is unacquainted with the abundance of our joys.

III. The Resemblance of Their Joy. To what may it be likened? The sacred writers have used various similitudes. It may be compared to the joy of the captive, released from bondage; to the joy of a patient, after his recovery from a severe illness; to the joy of a mariner, after a storm. Two figures are here employed to set forth the Christian's joy —

A. The joy of a husbandman in the field of harvest. "According to the joy of harvest."

1. It is a joy that results from labor.

2. Connected with anxiety.

3. Requires patience.

B. The joy of a soldier in the field of battle. "As men rejoice when they divide the spoil." It is a joy of end achieved, of anxiety relieved, of peace of mind attained.

Conclusion: This subject gives us a view of two things with regard to Christianity.

1. Its requirements. It is no easy thing. There is much to be done and suffered.

2. Its rewards. These are inestimable. Present and future — exceeding description and baffling conception.

— Ebenezer Temple

33. The Writing on God's Hand (Isa. 49:16)

These words are a singularly bold metaphor, drawn from the
strange and half-savage custom, which lingers still among sailors
and others, of having beloved names or other tokens of affection
and remembrance indelibly inscribed on parts of the body. Sometimes worshippers had the marks of the god thus set on their flesh;
here God writes on His hands the name of the city of His worshippers.

I. Here We Have Set Forth for Our Strength and
Peace a Divine Remembrance, More Tender Than a
Mother's (v. 15).

When Israel came out of Egypt, the Passover was instituted as
"a memorial unto all generations," or as the same idea is other-
wise expressed, "it shall be for a sign unto thee upon thine hand."
Here God represents Himself as doing for Israel what He had
bid Israel do for Him. They were, as it were, to write the supreme
act of deliverance in the Exodus upon their hands, that it might
never be forgotten. God writes Zion on His hands for the same
purpose.

The text does not primarily refer to individuals, but to the
community. But the recognition of that fact is not to be allowed
to rob us of the preciousness of this text in its bearing on the
individual. For God remembers the community, not as an abstrac-
tion or a generalised expression, but as the aggregate of all the
individuals composing it. We think of "the Church," and do not
think of the thousands of men and women who make it up. We
cannot discern the separate stars in the galaxy. But God's eye
resolves what to us is a nebula, and every single glittering point
of light hangs rounded and separate in the heaven. There is no
jostling nor confusion in the wide space of the heart of God. They
that go before shall not hinder them that come after.

That remembrance which each man may take for himself is
infinitely tender. The echo of the music of the previous words
still haunts the verse, and the remembrance promised in it is
touched with more than a mother's love. "I am poor and needy,"
says the Psalmist, "yet the Lord thinketh upon me." But do not
let us forget that it was a very sinful Zion that God thus remembered.

II. The Divine Remembrance Guides the Divine Action.
The palm of the hand is the seat of strength, of work; and so,

if Zion's name is written there, that means not only remembrance, but remembrance which is at the helm, as it were, which is moulding and directing all the work that is done by the hand that bears the name inscribed upon it.

For His Church, as a whole, He does more amidst the affairs of nations. You remember the grand words of one of the Psalms. He reproved kings for their sakes, saying, "Touch not Mine anointed, and do My prophets no harm." It is no fanatical reading of the history of earthly politics and kingdoms, if we recognize that one of the most prominent reasons for the divine activities in moulding the kingdoms, setting up and casting down, is the advancement of the Kingdom of heaven and the building of the City of God. "I have graven thee on the palms of My hands," and when the hands go to work, it is for the Zion whose likeness they bear.

But the same thing applies to us individually. "All things work together;" they would not do so, unless there was one dominant will which turned the chaos into a cosmos. "All things work together for my good."

III. The Divine Remembrance Works All Things, to Realise a Great Ideal End, As Yet Unreached.

"Thy walls are continually before Me." When this prophecy was uttered, the Israelites were in captivity, and the city was a wilderness; "the holy and beautiful house where the fathers praised Thee was burned with fire," the walls were broken down; rubbish and solitude were there. Yet on the palms of God's hands were inscribed the walls which were nowhere else! They were "before Him," though Jerusalem was a ruin.

It means that Divine remembrance sees "things that are not, as though they were." In the midst of the imperfect reality of the present condition of the Church as a whole, and of us, its actual components, it sees the ideal, the perfect vision of the perfect future. So, the most radiant optimism is the only fitting attitude for Christian people in looking into the future, either of the Church as a whole, or of themselves as individual members of it.

— Alexander Maclaren

34. Blaspheming God's Name (Isa. 52:5)

I. What Is Meant by the Name of the Lord? His perfections, titles, etc.

II. THE VARIOUS WAYS IN WHICH IT IS BLASPHEMED.

A. By denying His existence (Ps. 10:4; 14:1; 53:1).

B. By denying His sovereignty (Job 21:14, 15; Exod. 5:2).

C. By denying His truth (Gen. 3:4; Isa. 36:15; II Peter 3:3, 4).

D. By denying His power (II Kings 7:2; 15:30, 32-35; Ps. 78:19, 20).

E. By denying His omnipotence and omniscience (Job 22:13, 14; Ps. 10:11; 73:11; 94:7; Isa. 29:15; Ezek. 8:12).

F. By accusing Him of injustice (Jer. 12:1; Ezek. 18:25; 33:17; Mal. 2:17; 3:15).

G. By murmuring against His dispensations (Isa. 45:9; Exod. 14:11, 12).

H. By false swearing, oaths and curses, etc.

III. THE EXCUSES USUALLY MADE FOR IT. Ignorance, custom, example, surprise, passion, confirmation of what it said, meaning no harm, inconsistencies of professors, etc. (II Sam. 12:14; Ezek. 36:20; Rom. 2:24; II Peter 2:2).

IV. THE EVIL CONSEQUENCES OF IT. Destroys the little remains of the fear of God. Leads to the disobedience of all His commands. Sets a horrid example to others, especially to the young.

V. THE POWERFUL ARGUMENTS AGAINST IT. The Lord is our glorious and lawful Sovereign, who sees and hears all things. He is a holy and jealous God, before whose bar we must appear. He is fully able to punish and has assured us that He will (II Kings 19:22, 28; Isa. 37:23, 36-38; Ezek. 20:27, 33; 35:12-14).

— A. TUCKER

35. Lengthen and Strengthen (Isa. 54:2)

"Lengthen thy cords and strengthen thy stakes."

I. THE CHURCH MUST EVER BE LENGTHENING HER CORDS.

A. Expanding horizons.

B. Christ's kingdom must cover the earth.

C. "Go . . . into all the world . . . to every creature."

II. As We Lengthen the Cords We Must Strengthen the Stakes.

A. The taller the tree, the more rootage.

B. The higher the skyscraper, the deeper the foundation.

C. The more machinery, the larger must be the power plant.

D. The more we would do for Christ, the more we must seek His power and help.

36. The God of Nature (Jer. 5:24)

I. The Doctrine Asserted. "The Lord our God giveth . . ." He is the immediate Bestower of what we call natural benefits.

A. The Giver of rain.

1. He provides it in mercy to mankind.

2. He withholds it in judgment upon nations.

B. The Appointer of harvest. "He reserveth . . ." Important and interesting season. God has appointed it —

1. As an immutable ordinance (Gen. 8:22).

2. As a time of rejoicing.

3. As a means of instruction.

II. The Duty Inferred.

A. Cultivate continual acknowledgment of God.

B. Excercise entire dependence upon God.

C. Render perpetual thanksgiving to God.

D. Devote ourselves to the faithful service of God.

— H. Parr

37. The Duty of Self-Reflection (Lam. 3:40-42)

I. Its Usefulness.

A. Teaches us to know ourselves.

B. We discover our sins.

C. It provides good company and comfortable employment.

II. Its Neglect Damaging.

A. Hardens the heart.

B. A daily increase of sin.

C. Renders a man the more unwilling to reckon with himself.

III. Demands Diligence.

A. There is a natural reluctance to attend to the duty.

B. Many sins not easily discovered, unless diligent search is made.

C. A convenient time should be set apart for self-reflection.

D. Affliction a time for heart-searching.

E. Let not the difficulty of the work discourage you.

F. A work that must be often repeated.

IV. Leads to Repentance. "Turn again to the Lord." Sin is an aversion and turning away from God; repentance is a returning to Him.

A. Repentance must be speedy.

B. Thorough.

C. Resolute and steadfast.

— D. Conant

38. A Moral Resurrection (Ezek. 37:1-14)

I. The Multitude of Its Dead.

II. The Apparent Hopelessness of the Dead.

III. A Startling Command.

A. It is the Lord who speaks.

B. In His Words are —

1. Life.

2. Power.

IV. A Glorious Promise.

V. The Resurrection.

A. A noise.

B. A reunion.

C. Harmony in this reunion

D. Elastic strength for action.

E. A human form.

F. Life.

1. God, the Source.
2. The Spirit, the Agent.
3. His Word, the instrument.
4. Man, the medium.   — John Gill

39. Scripture Balances (Dan. 5:27)

I. In What Balances We Should Weigh Ourselves.

A. The balance of God's perfect law.

B. The balances of his blessed Gospel.

C. The balance even of our own conscience.

II. What lessons We Should Learn from Our Defects.

A. To be thankful for the Gospel.

B. To walk humbly before God.

C. To be preparing daily for the scrutiny that awaits us at the last day.   — Charles Simeon

40. The Spirit of the Lord's Espousals (Hos. 2:18, 19)

He declares by what means He would "betroth them to Him forever;" even in righteousness and judgment, and then in kindness and mercies, and then in faithfulness.

God had indeed from the beginning covenanted with the Israelites:

I. "In Righteousness and in Judgment." There is nothing disguised or false in His covenant. As then God had in sincerity adopted the people. To what vices does He oppose righteousness and judgment? I answer, These words must be applied to both the contracting parties; then by righteousness God means not only His own, but that also which is, as they say, mutual and reciprocal. And by "righteousness and judgment" He means rectitude in which nothing is lacking. Let us take this to heart.

II. "In Kindness and Mercies." By these words He intimates that though the people were unworthy, yet this would be no impediment in their way to prevent them to return into favor with God; for in this reconciliation God would regard His own goodness rather than the merits of His people.

III. "In Faithfulness." This confirms the fixed and unchangeable duration of the marriage. By faithfulness is to be understood that stability of which I have spoken. We embrace God's free promises, and thus the covenant the Lord makes with us is ratified. And is forever sure.   — John Calvin

41. The Spoiled Cake (Hos. 7:2)

Hosea's composition is epigrammatic and figurative. He compares Ephraim to "a silly dove," easily enticed into the net. When frightened, will not stay in the cot where she is safe. To "a wild ass alone" — foolish, headstrong, wilful. "An empty vine" — fruitless and useless. "A child" tenderly brought up, who turns out rebellious. "A merchant," deceitful in his balances. "A cake not turned," which, for want of turning is burnt on one side, and dough on the other side, but good for nothing on either side. Israel was not completely consecrated to God.

I. God Demands the Consecration of Man's Entire Being. The cake should have been baked on both sides. Body, soul, time, possessions, should all be devoted to God. He claims it. The claim is based on —

A. What God is in Himself.

B. What He is relative to Us.

C. Our highest interests.

II. Some Consecrate to God only a Portion of Their Being. Baked on one side only. This indicates —

A. Self-will.

B. Lack of supreme love to God.

C. Aversion to submission.

D. Love of present pleasure.

E. Ignorance of the ease of religious service.

F. Indecision of character.

III. The Consecration of only a Portion of Our Being to God Will End in Destruction. It is destructive of —

A. Complete devotion.

B. Force of character.

C. True usefulness.

D. Thorough enjoyment.
E. Final perseverance.
F. Future glory.

— B. D. Johns

42. Alarm in God's House (Joel 2:1)

I. A Sacred Scene.

II. Our Places of Worship May be Designated Holy Mountains.

A. Because there a holy God is worshipped.

B. Because there holy gifts are imparted.

C. Because there holy anticipations are realised.

III. A Solemn Warning. Against —

A. Formality in the exercises of religion.

B. Conformity to the world.

C. Deadness to the power of prayer.

D. Inactivity in the cause of Christ.

— Ebenezer Temple

43. Preparation to Meet God (Amos 4:12)

I. To Whom May This Command Be Considered as Addressed? All who have made no preparation for meeting God.

A. Those who have intentionally crowded the whole subject from their minds.

B. Those who have deferred the subject with an intention to prepare at a future time. They have some sense of the importance and necessity of making preparation.

C. Those who spend their time in preparing for other things, so as to crowd this subject out, though without any specific or settled intention of doing so.

D. Those who have given some slight attention to the subject, but have settled down on that which will, in fact, constitute no preparation when they come to appear before God. They are relying on some delusive views and hopes, some erroneous doctrine or opinions; some vague, unsettled, and unsubstantial feelings. These classes embrace a large portion of the human family.

II. Why Should Preparation Be Made to Meet God?

A. Because it is to be our first interview with Him face to face.

B. Because we shall meet Him in very solemn circumstances.

C. Because we go there on a very calm errand.

D. Because God has solemnly commanded such preparation.

E. Because when we are brought before Him, it will be too late to do what is necessary to be done.

III. What Is Necessary to Be Done in Order to Be Prepared to Meet God?

Mere bravery or courage is not a preparation to meet God. Not more prepared to meet God is he who bids defiance to death. Nor is studied insensibility in death the proper preparation.

A. It is necessary to be reconciled to God. No one is prepared to meet Him to whom He is a stranger or a foe.

B. It is necessary to be born again; to be renewed by the Holy Ghost.

C. There must be true repentance for sin, and true faith in the Lord Jesus Christ. The sum of what I say is this, To be prepared to meet God, we must comply exactly with what He requires. We must meet His terms. No one need ever to have made any mistake on this point.

IV. When We Should Prepare to Meet God.

We must attend to it today; we must defer it no longer. The Bible requires it to be done at once; it demands that everything else should give way for it; that this day may end your probation; and that there is slender probability of preparation being made on a dying bed. — Albert Barnes

44. The Church Delivered, Purified, and Privileged
(Obad. 17-20)

I. The Deliverance of the Church of God. Mount Zion signifies the Church, the entire mass of those who are given to the Lord Jesus Christ, and whom He has ransomed by His blood. It is remarkable that what is exhibited as the liberation of the Church is always conjoined with the destruction of some opposing power. The fact is, the destruction of the opposing power is the means used for the liberating of the Church. Conquest in the world is triumph in the Church. Consolation is combined with liberation. Deliverance is the first and principal object which presented itself to the mind of the Lord Jesus. His death was a necessary step to His resurrection, His resurrection to His exaltation, His exaltation to the assumption of His mediatorial power. We see that Jesus Christ first fought and conquered, and then He became the liberator of the world. In the world He works liberation by instrumentality, and the great agency employed in carrying it on is the Holy Spirit. Liberation begins with Christ, but it does not end with Him; for, as He Himself obtained resurrection by the power of God, so there is another resurrection which takes place in the breast of every man who is the subject of His kingdom.

II. The Grand Effect Which the Text Sets Forth. "There shall be holiness." The mount of deliverance is always the mount of holiness. Another name for holiness is spiritual health. Bring the whole to this one point, that the test of state is character; that wherever this holiness is met with, there the deliverance that has been effected on Mount Zion by the Lord Jesus is applied, and there the liberation that the Spirit of God works in the souls of His people is likewise brought to pass.

III. The Privileges to Which This Effect Leads, and for Which It Prepares. "Shall possess their possessions." Canaan for the earlier saints. For us "the inheritance of the saints."   — John Campbell

45. The Knell of Nineveh (Jonah 3:4)

I. The Precision and Punctuality of the Divine Arrangement. God knew exactly the day when Nineveh's lease of mercy should end. He has determined the length of endurance of our sin.

II. Religious Warning May Seem Preposterous. To many still it is more a joke than anything else. Men boast of their health, but I have noticed that it is often the invalids who live long. "In such an hour as ye think not, the Son of Man cometh."

III. God Gives Every Man a Fair Chance for His Life. The iniquity of Nineveh was accumulating. Why did not God unsheath some sword of lightning from the scabbard of a storm-cloud and slay it? It was because He wanted to give the city a fair chance. And God is giving us a fair chance for safety, a better chance for safety, a better chance than He gave to Nineveh. (Of course, we are here speaking after the manner of men.)

IV. When the People Repent, God Lets Them Off. While Nineveh was on its knees, God reversed the judgment. When a sinner repents (in one sense) God repents (in another). Then repent, give up your sin and turn to God, and you will be saved.

— T. DeWitt Talmage

46. Christ the Breaker (Mic. 2:13)

I. The Great Work of Our Divine Redeemer, by Which He Has Broken for the Captives the Prison-House of Their Bondage. Many of us know not the bondage in which we are held. We are chained by sin, chained by the habit of evil with a strength of which you never know till you try to shake off.

II. Jesus Christ as the Opener, and the Path, to God. Our condition is not only one of bondage to evil, but also one of separation from God. We do not know God as He is, except by Jesus Christ. It is only the God manifest in Jesus Christ that draws men's hearts to Him. That God that is in Christ is the only God that humanity ever loved. He, by the fact of His Cross and Passion, has borne and borne away the impediments of our own sin and transgression which rise for ever between us and Him, unless He shall sweep them out of the way.

III. Christ Is the Breaker as the Captain of Our Life's March. "When He putteth forth His sheep, He goeth before them."

IV. He Is the Breaker for Us of the Bands of Death. Christ's resurrection is the only solid proof of a future life. It is not possible that we should be holden of the impotent chains that He has broken. — Alexander Maclaren

47. National Punshments Part of God's Moral Government (Nah. 1:2)

I. The Certainty that Sin Will Not Remain Unpunished.

A. The inevitable working of natural laws secures this. Physical, social, and spiritual evils follow sin.

B. The declared character of God secures it. He is a jealous God.

II. There Is No Resisting the Judgments of God. His power is seen in nature. The rolling whirlwind, the dark tempest, the desolating storm are symbols of His wrath and of His might.

III. Yet in Wrath God Remembers Mercy.

A. There is a refuge for those who turn and repent.

B. No sins preclude hope.

C. Salvation is full and certain to the truly penitent.

D. Though the godly suffer trouble, they will be delivered from it. Their trials are only a discipline, if used aright.

— C. Cunningham Geikie

48. Self-Conceit (Hab. 1:10)

The over-estimate of one's capabilities and powers, and the depreciation of the capabilities and powers of all other people. Self-knowledge is not self-conceit. Nor is the right and diligent use of the talents with which God has entrusted us any indication of self-conceit. Illustration — The principle contained in the words, "They sacrifice unto their own net . . ."

I. Men Do This When They Attribute Their Temporal Prosperity to Their Own Skill and Energy, and Not to God. Wealth may, or may not, be a proof of skill and industry. Self-reliance is a noble quality; it is different from self-sufficiency. But we are dependent upon God.

II. When They Attribute the Discoveries of Science and the Inventions that Have Benefited the World to the Human Intellect and Not to God. Man's discoveries are God's revelations.

III. When They Attribute the Prosperity of a Country to Any Other Source Than to God. Patriotism is a virtue. Our prosperity may be ascribed to different causes. Let us honor God; let not our pride weaken us.

IV. In Their Treatment of God's Merciful Revelation to the World.

V. WHEN THEY DEPEND FOR THE SPREAD OF GOD'S RULE ON HUMAN PLANS AND ORGANIZATIONS, AND NOT ON THE BLESSING OF THE HIGHEST. "The excellency of the power is of God." Without God's presence and blessing all that we do is in vain.

— JAMES OWEN

49. Practical Atheism in Denying the Agency of God's Providence (Zeph. 1:12)

Practical atheism brought the judgments of God upon the Jews. These were fully executed in the Babylonish Captivity. By being "settled on their lees" we may understand their riches; for wine grows rich by being kept on the lees. So, by a long scene of peace and prosperity, the inhabitants of Jerusalem were arriving at very great riches. Or it may signify a state of security; like wine settled on the lees, they have been undisturbed. "I will punish" should be "I will visit." The charge here brought against the Jews amounts to this — that their temper and practice were such as would not at all agree to the practical belief of a Providence. They thought and acted as if it were their real and professed belief that the Lord would do neither good nor evil, nor meddle with human affairs. This atheistical affectation of independency, and secret or practical renunciation of divine Providence, is the fatal thing that generally overturned the empires, and improverished, enslaved, and ruined the nations of the earth.

I. THE DOCTRINE OF A DIVINE PROVIDENCE. Maybe you already speculatively believe this doctrine, but the grand defect lies in the efficacy of this belief on your hearts and lives. We may argue from the perfections of God, and His relations to us. We may argue from our confessed obligations to religion and the worship of God. The testimony of Scripture is plain. New and unexpected witnesses may be found in the heathen, — such as Nebuchadnezzar, Cyrus, Plato, Horace, Cicero, and various poets and philosophers.

II. THINGS IN TEMPER AND CONDUCT WHICH ARGUE A SECRET AND PRACTICAL DISBELIEF OF THE DOCTRINE OF PROVIDENCE.

A. Would there be so little prayer among us, if we were generally affected with this truth?

B. Is not the general indulgence of vice, and neglect of religion, a plain evidence of the general disbelief in a divine providence over the country?

C. Is not the general impenitence, notwithstanding the many public calamities under which our country has groaned, a sad evidence of this practical atheism?

D. Is not the general ingratitude a plain evidence of the general disbelief of a providential government over the world?

E. How little serious and humble acknowledgment of the providence of God in our disappointments and mortifications is to be found among us!

III. THE WICKEDNESS OF THIS ATHEISTICAL TEMPER AND CONDUCT. To deny the agency of profidence is the most daring rebellion against the King of heaven; it is to abjure His government in His own territories, in His own world which He has made. What unnatural ingratitude! What intolerable pride and arrogance! What impiety and insolence! This atheistical spirit is the source of all vice and irreligion.   — SAMUEL DAVIES

50. The Nations Shaken and the Desire of All Come
(Hag. 2:6-7)

Three things are foretold in this remarkable prediction.

1. Great commotions and tribulations in the earth.

2. Wonderful and unexpected revolutions.

3. The glorious and happy issue of all these commotions, in the final triumph of Christ and His Gospel. He is properly called the "desire of all nations," because the whole creation groans for deliverance from guilt, for an interposing Mediator, who can make atonement for sin, satisfy divine justice, and give peace to a wounded conscience. To Christ, therefore, and to His religion, this prophecy belongs.

I. TEXT REFERS TO THE PERIOD WHEN JESUS WAS MANIFESTED IN THE FLESH. To prepare the way for this grand event, we may see the omnipotent Jehovah shaking the heavens, earth, and seas.

II. VIEW TEXT AS RECEIVING ITS ACCOMPLISHMENT IN OUR OWN DAY.

A. He is shaking many kingdoms by awful judgments and unexpected revolutions. Concerning the shaking of the nations, note three things —

1. They are from God.

2. To the nations visited, the judgments of God are in wrath, and correctors of iniquity.

3. The effect of these visitations will be either unfeigned repentance and reformation, or utter ruin and destruction.

B. Though the shaking of the nations bring deserved calamity on guilty lands, yet the final issue of all will be the wide extent of our glorious Redeemer's kingdom, and the universal triumph of His Gospel. These predictions are now being fulfilled. All these present tumults and desolations are connected with events which shall bring peace, and righteousness, and joy to the whole earth.

— Andrew A. Bonar

51. Nothing Trifling (Zech. 4:10)

"Who hath despised the day of small things?"

I. Natural Trifles Yielding Great Results.
The seed; the spark; the mountain stream; the child.

II. Providential Trifles Issuing in Great Lives.
Joseph, Moses, Daniel.

III. Historical Trifles Producing Great Revolutions.

A. Introduction of the gospel.

B. The Reformation.

C. Denominational beginnings.

D. Missionary enterprises.   — W. W. Wythe

52. The Divine Refiner (Mal. 3:3)

In the preceding verse, Christ is a refiner's fire, but in this He is the refiner sitting and watching the metal in the fire. His position suggests —

I. That His People Need Refining. The dross of sin cleaves to the holiest. Nothing cleaves so closely. Christ sees dross where we do not. We are not always willing that it should be purged away when we do see it. The furnace is necessary.

II. That His People Are Being Refined. They find life a fiery ordeal. They often suffer more than sinners. The heat is often very penetrating; sometimes very hard to bear with patience. They do not always recognise the purpose of suffering. The process goes on even when the results are not perceived. A refiner's furnace is the truest simile of life.

III. That His People Are Valuable In His Eyes. He watches them in the furnace. He waits for their perfection. They are silver, not common earth. Often despised by the world, they are highly esteemed by Him. The refiner only watches precious metals in the fire. "Reprobate silver" may be consumed, but every particle of pure metal is preserved. Christ's people are precious to Him.

IV. That His People Will Have Their Fiery Trials Tempered to Their Spiritual Requirements. He aims to make them spiritually perfect. He tempers the fire that He may separate "the sin that He hates from the souls that He loves." He seeks not to give carnal enjoyment, but purity. He, sitting to watch, manifests solicitude, patience, expectancy, and care.

V. That in the End His People Will Be Fully Purified. His purpose shall be accomplished in them. We often see the purification going on. The refiner uses the silver he purifies. Perfect purity will bring perfect blessedness.

Learn —

1. To trust more perfectly the watchful care of your Refiner under your trials.

2. To estimate your trials by the amount of purifying they accomplish.

3. To co-operate with the refiner in His efforts to purify you.

— W. Osborne Lilley

53. Come Unto Me (Matt. 11:28)

"Come unto me, all ye that labor and are heavy laden, and I will give you rest."

I. The Characteristics of the Speaker.

A. He is sympathetic.

B. He is conscious of all-efficiency in His person and work.

D. He is urgent.

C. He is untiring (as fresh today as ever).

E. He is meek, and lowly in heart.

II.   THE UNIVERSALITY OF HIS APPEAL.

A. All mankind are included.

B. Every age and rank.

C. The Son of Man above all tribal and racial distinctions.

III.   THE RESPONSE IT DEMANDS.

A. It must be personal.

B. It should be immediate.

C. It may be unemotional.   — F. B. MEYER

54. The Food of the World (Matt. 14:19, 20)

I.   CHRIST FEEDS THE FAMISHING WORLD BY MEANS OF HIS CHURCH. "He gave the loaves to His disciples, and the disciples to the multitude."

A. The food, although supernaturally provided, is carried to the hungry by the ordinary means; the disciples gave it to the multitude.

B. The disciples were prepared for their work. The first lesson they had to learn was the almost ludicrous disproportion between the means at their command and the necessities of the crowd. "How many loaves have ye? Go and see."

C. We must carry our poor and inadequate resources to Christ. "Bring them hither to me."

II.   THE BREAD IS ENOUGH FOR ALL THE WORLD. "They did all eat, and were filled."

III.   THE BREAD WHICH IS GIVEN TO THE FAMISHING IS MULTIPLIED FOR THE FUTURE OF THE DISTRIBUTORS. "They took of the fragments that remained twelve baskets full."
                                      — ALEXANDER MACLAREN

55. How to Meet Offences (Matt. 18:15-18)

Observe the method Christ has laid down.

I. The Trespass Supposed, Whether Accidental or Designed. Whether it regards reputation, or property or feelings, etc. Then, the direction given —

II. Seek a Private Interview. That he may explain, if possible. Better adapted for him to confess. More faithfully and affectionately admonished.

III. If This Fail, Take One or Two More. Let them be unobjectionable, peaceable, prudent persons. They are to witness and aid by their counsel and influence. If this fail —

IV. Bring It to the Church. Do so for these reasons:
A. For the offender's sake. He may hear the Church.
B. For Christianity's sake.
C. For the world's sake, that they may see we are neither indifferent or malevolent. If he refuse to hear the Church, then he must —

V. Be Removed from Christian Communion. This is the last act, and if this is rightly done, it is ratified in heaven (verse 18). Do not neglect this order. You object, "He is not worthy of all this;" "This is troublesome," etc. But it is your duty; Christ demands it.   — Jabez Burns

56. The Talents (Matt. 25:22, 23)

I. God Bestows Gifts on Every Man According to His Own Sovereign Will.
A. God is the source and author of every blessing we enjoy.
B. He dispenses extremely various gifts to various persons.
C. These he bestows according to his own sovereign will.

II. He Will Reward Every Man, Not So Much According to the Talents He Possesses, as According to His Fidelity in Improving Them.
A. A man, endued with great gifts, will not be the more approved on that account.

B. Nor will a person of the smallest talents be on that account overlooked.

C. The Scriptures speak strongly upon each of these points. Infer:

1. What little reason is there to envy those who have great talents.

2. How earnest should every one be in trading with the talent committed to him.

3. How little should we regard the attempts of the ungodly to repress our zeal.   — CHARLES SIMEON

57. A Parable Concerning Our Lord as the Bread of Life (Mark 8:1-9)

I. OUR LORD MEETS SIMILAR NEEDS.

A. The multitudes were in a desert place.

B. The needs of the multitude could not be met by human capacity.

C. The need of the multitude was the common need of all.

II. OUR LORD OFTEN PROVIDES BY THE SAME METHODS.

A. He uses ordinary things as agencies of blessing.

B. He employs His disciples as benefactors.

III. OUR LORD MANIFESTS THE SAME CARE AND MAJESTY.

A. Note Christ's Care.

1. He observes their hunger.

2. He notices their weariness. Hence He finds for them the resting place of green grass. There is the same care in His provision, for all varied wants, in the Gospel, and, perhaps, in the very divisions of the Church.

3. He abundantly meets their needs. Seven baskets left.

B. Note Christ's Majesty.

1. There is the dignity of calmness. No perturbation in His manner or tone.

2. There is the royalty of command. Both to the disciples and the crowd He speaks with authority that inspires confidence and ensures obedience.

3. There is the divinity of the supernatural. So with souls, Christ is the Royal Redeemer. "Thy king cometh unto thee."

— Urijah R. Thomas

58. The Widow's Mites (Mark 12:41-44)

I. Some of the Things Which the Incident Reveals Concerning Christ Himself.

A. It presents Him as the omniscient Searcher of hearts.

B. By what a different standard Christ judges men's actions from that they themselves judge by.

C. His eyes are upon the treasury and those who contribute to it.

II. Some of the Things Which this Incident Reveals Respecting Ourselves.

A. It shows that offerings to the Lord's treasury must bear some decent proportion to what He has bestowed upon us.

B. Our offerings to be acceptable must be felt to involve some sacrifice.

C. Liberality is a means of grace.

III. There Are Here Lessons for the Whole Church.

A. What value God sets on titles.

B. Christ will strictly hold the Church to account for all the wealth bestowed upon her.   — James Moir

59. A Model of a Happy Married Life (Luke 1:6)

I. The Spirit's Testimony to the Truthfulness of Their Inner Life.

A. The character they attained: "They were both *righteous*."

B. The similarity of their distinction: "They were *both* righteous."

C. The reality of their devotion: "Righteous *before God*."

II. The Spirit's Testimony to the Consistency of Their Outward Life.

A. They were diligent in religion: "*Walking*."

B. They were obedient to the laws of God: "Walking *in all the commandments.*"

C. They were attentive to the religious rites of their day: "Walking *in all the commandments and ordinances.*"

D. They were complete in their service: "Walking in *all* the commandments and ordinances."

E. They were faultless in their characters: *"Blameless."*
— PASQUIER QUESNEL

60. Christian Mercy (Luke 6:36)

I. THE NATURE OF CHRISTIAN MERCY.

A. It has its seat in the heart.

B. It is a supernatural quality.

C. It is an active principle.

1. It will be manifested toward the inferior animals.

2. To those of our fellow-creatures who are under bodily affliction and misery.

3. It will extend to the spiritual miseries of our fellow-men. Mercy to the soul, is the soul of mercy.

4. Towards our greatest enemies.

II. THE GROUNDS OF CHRISTIAN MERCY.

A. It is strictly enjoined by God.

B. We stand in constant need of divine mercy. Were it withdrawn, there would be nothing before us but a fearful looking for of judgment.

C. Our profession binds us to imitate Christ, who is the perfect pattern of mercy. In Him mercy was embodied. If we are His disciples, we will walk even as He walked.

D. We should be merciful because of the true pleasure which is associated with acts of mercy.

E. It is an express condition of our obtaining mercy.

III. THE REWARDS OF CHRISTIAN MERCY.

A. A good name.

B. A peculiar interest in the kind and merciful arrangements of divine providence.

C. The merciful are blessed with the prayers and blessings of the miserable whom they have relieved.

D. They shall be blessed with the public approval of Christ at the last day.

Application:

A. Let the exercise of mercy be emphasized to all Christ's disciples. Cultivate it. Rejoice in all opportunities of doing good.

B. Let the mercy of God to us be highly valued. We need it daily. There is only one channel for its communication — through Christ. Only one way to obtain it — through faith in His word.

C. The unmerciful shall have judgment without mercy. What a dreadful portion to the guilty sinner!   — JABEZ BURNS

61. At His Feet (Luke 7:36-50)

I.   IT IS A BECOMING POSTURE.

A. As He is divine, let us pay Him lowliest reverence.

B. As we are sinful, let us make humble confession.

C. As He is Lord, let us make full submission.

D. As He is All in All, let us manifest immovable dependence.

E. As He is infinitely wise, let us wait His appointed time. The best are at His feet, joyfully bowing before Him. The worst must come there whether they will or no.

II.   IT IS A HELPFUL POSTURE.

A. For a weeping penitent (Luke 7:38).

B. For a resting convert (8:35).

C. For a pleading intercessor (8:41).

D. For a willing learner (10:39).

E. For a grateful worshipper (17:16).

F. For a saint beholding his Lord's glory (Rev. 1:17).

III.   IT IS A SAFE POSTURE.

A. Jesus will not refuse us in that position, for it is one which we ought to occupy.

B. Jesus will not spurn the humbly submissive, who in self-despair cast themselves before Him.

C. Jesus will not suffer any to harm those who seek refuge at His feet.

D. Jesus will not deny us the eternal privilege of abiding there. Let this be our continual posture — sorrowing or rejoicing, hoping or fearing, suffering or working, teaching or learning, in secret or in public, in life and in death.   — Charles H. Spurgeon

62. Christ Receiving Sinners (Luke 15:1, 2)

I. The Description of Sinners Christ will Receive.

A. Sinners of all ages.

B. Sinners of all stations.

C. Sinners of all degrees.

II. Into What Jesus Receives Sinners.

A. Into His forgiving grace and favor.

B. Into His family.

C. Into His heaven.

III. The Way and Manner in Which Christ Receives Sinners.

A. In the way of acknowledgment and confession.

B. In the way of repentance, or turning from sin.

C. In the way of humility and faith. Now as to the manner:

1. Most freely.

2. Most tenderly.

3. Most readily.

Application:

1. The subject is one to which every believer's heart responds.

2. The subject is full of encouragement to the inquiring sinner.

3. The subject is limited to the present life. Here only He receives.   — Jabez Burns

63. The Dying Robber Saved

I. Consider the Previous Character of This Man.

A. He was not a pagan, but a Jew — a believer in the true God.

B. A believer in future existence and retribution.

C. He had become a hardened wretch.

II.   NOTICE HIS TRUE REPENTANCE. This is evidenced —

A. In his viewing sin in its relation to God.

B. In his acknowledgment of his own guilt.

C. In his reproving the conduct of the other robber, and his anxiety for his welfare.

III.   HIS STRONG FAITH. He believed —

A. That Christ had a kingdom.

B. That He would hear requests.

C. That He would grant blessings.

IV.   HIS PRAYER.

A. Short; but a single sentence.

B. Humble; he only asked to be remembered.

C. Reliant. Remember all my past bad life; but remember, too, that I am dying trusting in Thy grace.

D. Earnest. The petition of an awakened sinner on the brink of eternity.

E. Comprehensive. It included all he needed.

V.   CHRIST'S ANSWER.

Conclusions:

1. If Christ heard prayer when passing through His awful suffering upon the cross, will He not hear now that He is exalted to be a Prince and a Savior?

2. The conversion of this man shows how quickly Christ can save.

3. Salvation is all of grace, and not of works or merit.

4. Christ can not only justify and give us a title to heaven in a short time; He can also quickly sanctify and make us "meet to be partakers of the inheritance of the saints in light."

5. One robber was taken and the other left.

6. This is the only case of death-bed conversion recorded in the Bible.   — JOHN L. CAMPBELL

64. Christ Giving Up His Spirit to the Father
(Luke 23:46)

I. THE HUMAN SPIRIT SURVIVES THE DISSOLUTION OF THE BODY.

A. True philosophy renders this highly probable.

B. The Bible reveals it as an incontrovertible fact.

II. THE GLORY OF HUMAN NATURE CONSISTS IN BEING WITH THE FATHER.

A. To guide me in my endless course.

B. To supply the wants of my imperishable being.

III. THE ATTAINMENT OF THIS GLORY INVOLVES THE VOLUNTARY COMMITMENT OF MAN TO GOD.

A. To be ruled by His holy law.

B. To be employed in His blessed service.

IV. THIS VOLUNTARY COMMITMENT GIVES MORAL GRANDEUR TO DEATH.

A. This makes death, not a conquest, but a victory (I Cor. 15:57).

B. This makes our departure, not a calamity, but an "entrance," which shall be ministered unto us "abundantly into the everlasting kingdom of our Lord and Savior Jesus Christ" (II Peter 1:11).

— CALEB MORRIS

65. The Mission of John and of Christ (John 1:6)

I. THE TRUE NATURE OF A CHRISTIAN MINISTER'S OFFICE.

A. Ministers are not priests or mediators.

B. They are not agents into whose hands men may commit their souls, and carry on their religion by deputy.

C. They are witnesses (Acts 1:8, 2:40; 20:21).

II. ONE PRINCIPAL POSITION WHICH OUR LORD OCCUPIES TOWARDS MANKIND. As light.

A. He is the center and source of all spiritual illumination, warmth, life, health, growth, beauty, and fertility.

B. He shines for the common benefit of mankind — for high and low, rich and poor, Jew and Greek.

C. He is free to all.

III. The Desperate Wickedness of Man's Natural Heart.

A. Christ was in the world invisibly long before He was born (Col. 1 :17). Yet He was neither known nor honored.

B. But Christ came visibly into the world when He was born at Bethlehem and fared no better. His own rejected Him.

IV. The Vast Privileges of All Who Receive Christ and Believe on Him.

A. The privileges are those of children.

B. These privileges are to be possessed by faith (Gal. 1 :26).

C. Are we sons of God? Have we the marks of Sonship.

D. Do we desire to be sons of God? Then we must receive Him as Savior.   — John C. Ryle

66. The Father's Love (John 16:26, 27)

I. Its Nature.

A. A redeeming love. "God so loved the world . . ."

B. A calling love. "No man cometh unto Me except the Father draw him."

C. An adopting love. "Behold what manner of love . . ."

D. A protecting love. Babes, children, want guardian care, "Can a mother forget . . ."

E. A sanctifying love. As we all desire to see our children grow, so our Father desires to se us grow in grace. "Whom the Lord loveth, He chasteneth."

F. An everlasting love (Jer. 31).

II. Its Claims. "My Son, give Me Thy heart."

A. Supreme love — a love of Him above every creature whatsoever.

B. Practical love (chap. 14 :21; I John 3 :18).

C. Expansive love. It must embrace all God's family for His sake. Apply this in the way of —

1. Reproof.

2. Encouragement.   — Montagu Villiers

67. The Ascension (Acts 1:9-12)

I. THE LORD WAS TAKEN UP INTO HEAVEN.

A. Fact of the ascension: stated here (Luke 24; Acts 1.)

B. Also implied — e.g., John 6:62; 20:17.

C. And in Acts and Epistles asserted — e.g., Eph. 4:10; I Tim. 3:16; I Peter 3:22. Also in the Acts and Epistles, implied (the Savior being ever referred to as living, invisible, glorified, and to come again from heaven). (See, e.g., Acts 7:55, 56; Phil. 3:20; I Thes. 4:16.)

D. 1. An absolute miracle.

2. And also a consoling and teaching truth, in what it says of the reality of heaven and as aiding us in grasping that reality (Col. 3:1). Heaven is where He is.

II. HE SAT ON THE RIGHT HAND OF GOD.

A. The metaphor (from an Oriental throne, a seat admitting more than one occupant) implies the share of the incarnate Lord in the supreme glory — more than mere nearness to it.

B. See, in support of this, Rev. 22:1, etc. ("throne of God and of the Lamb") ; and especially John 17:5.

C. Reflect — "the Son of Man (chap. 7:55) is at the right hand of God." Not only is Christ there as God the Son (John 1:1, etc.), but as man — as Jesus (Acts 1:11; Heb. 4:14). What a pledge for His brethren (John 17:24, etc.)

III. AFTER THAT HE HAD SPOKEN TO THEM.

A. Merciful prelude. The clear, spoken revelation given before the mysterious removal. We see Him not (I Peter 1:8), but He has spoken —

1. In human speech.

2. In visible life.

3. In atoning death (see Heb. 12:24).

B. Application of this and the whole ascension truth (John 17:13). He has spoken. He is there.   — GEORGE E. MOULE

68. Mighty in the Scriptures (Acts 18:23)

I. IN THE STUDY OF THE SCRIPTURES. This must be —
A. Systematic.
B. Thorough.
C. Oft-repeated.
D. With all the aid that outside sources can afford.
E. Prayerful and with dependence on the guide into all truth.

II. IN THE KNOWLEDGE OF THE SCRIPTURES (as following from the former). In the knowledge of their —
A. History.
B. Doctrine.
C. Ethics.
D. End and aim.

III. IN THE EXPOSITION OF THE SCRIPTURES (as following from both the first and the second).
A. In the opening up of their meaning.
B. In the ready and apt quotation of texts.
C. In the application of the truth to the heart and conscience.

IV. IN THE EFFECTS WHICH THE MIGHTY STUDY, KNOWLEDGE AND EXPOSITION OF THE SCRIPTURES ARE CALCULATED TO PRODUCE. "Mightily grew the Word of God and prevailed."
A. In the edification of the Church.
B. In the multiplication of converts.

— JABEZ BURNS

69. Law and Faith, The Two Great Moral Forces in Human History (Romans 3:29-31)

"The law" means that which is written in every man's soul, and republished on Sinai. "Faith" means the gospel, "the glad tidings" of sovereign love to a ruined world. These two great moral forces of the world may be looked upon in three aspects.

I. AS AGREEING IN SOME RESPECTS.
A. In authorship. Both are divine.
B. In spirit. Love is the moral essence, the inspiration of both.

C. In purpose. The well-being of humanity is the ultimate aim of both.

II. As Differing in Some Features.

A. One is older in human history than the other. The law is as old as the human soul. The gospel began with man after the Fall (Gen. 3:15).

B. One addresses man as a creature, the other as a sinner. Law comes to him as ruined sinner, and the gospel offers him assistance and restoration.

C. The one speaks imperatively, the other with compassion. "Thou shalt," "Thou shalt not," is the voice of law. The gospel invites, "Let the wicked forsake his way;" "Come unto Me;" "Ho, every one that thirsteth."

D. The "law" demands, the "gospel" delivers. The law says, Do this and that, or Desist from this or that, and will hear no excuse. The gospel comes and offers deliverance from the morally feeble and condemned state into which man has fallen.

III. As Co-operating to One Result.
The law prepares for the gospel by carrying the conviction of sin and ruin. The gospel exalts and enthrones the law. This is the point of the text, "Do we then make void the law through faith? God forbid." How does the gospel establish the law?

A. It presents it to man in the most commanding aspects.

B. It enthrones it in the soul.

C. It glorifies it in the life.

— David Thomas

70. Fervent In Spirit (Romans 12:11)

I. What Is It to be Fervent in Spirit? To be serious and earnest in —

A. The exercise of graces; in our —

1. Love to God (Deut. 6:5; Matt. 22:37).
2. Desire of Him (Psa. 42:1, 2).
3. Trust in Him (Job 13:25).
4. Rejoicing in Him (I Peter 1:8).

5. Zeal for His glory (I Cor. 10:31), which yet must be —
  (a) Tempered with knowledge (chap. 10:2).
  (b) Regulated by His Word.
6. Repentance (Job 42:5, 6).
7. Faith in Christ (James 2:26).
B. The performance of duties in —
1. Prayer (I Cor. 14:15).
2. Hearing (Ezek. 33:31).
3. Meditation (Psa. 22).

II. Why Thus Fervent in Spirit?

A. The end of God's giving us such active spirits is that we might employ them for Him (Prov. 16:4).

B. These are businesses of the greatest concern (Deut. 30:15).

C. Whatsoever is not done fervently is no good work (Eccl. 9:10).

Conclusions:

A. Bewail your former indiffernce.

B. Be more serious for the future.

Consider —

A. Good works are great works you perform (II Cor. 2:16).

B. You cannot be too serious in them (Luke 17:10).

C. Heaven will recompense all your labors (I Cor. 15:58).

— William Beveridge

71. A Pastor's Parting Blessing (Romans 16:21-24)

Long has this benediction lain in the Epistle like the wheat in the Egyptian tomb, but there is a vitality in it yet; lo, it buds and brings forth good to us after the lapse of eighteen centuries.

I. What Is Meant by the Grace of Our Lord Jesus Christ?

A. The grace which was revealed in Christ.

B. The grace which comes to us through Christ. Our Lord, as it were, took out of the river-bed of grace the great rock which blocked up the water-courses.

C. The grace which comes to us with Christ. Peculiar and abundant blessings come to souls who abide in Christ.

D. All the grace that is in any way connected with Christ. Elsewhere he extends the benediction to the love of God and the communion of the Holy Ghost. But the shorter form is intended to comprehend all the rest. In many of his epistles the apostle sums up with "grace be with you all," without mentioning any person of the Godhead. So that "the grace of our Lord Jesus Christ" is synonymous with grace as such; and comprehends all the various displays of grace. He wishes the saints all the grace they need, or can desire and that the Infinite God can give.

E. When the text is the desire of our heart, we mean —

1. May the love of Jesus Christ be with you, and may you know that you have it.

2. May His mercy be with you, as shown by the full pardon of all your sins, and your knowledge of it.

3. May you be the subjects of His work constantly.

4. May you have His peace.

5. May you exhibit the grace which shone so brightly in Him, and was seen by men and angels to the glory of God the Father.

II. With Whom is This Grace to Be?

A. With all the saints.

1. You all need it.

2. You all may have it.

3. There is no grace which you may not have, and which you ought to be content to go without. It is grievous to see how we stunt ourselves, and appear content with a poor form of spiritual life.

B. All the saints, i.e. —

1. Church officers.

2. Church workers.

3. Church members, poor, rich, young, and old.

C. This benediction is limited to the saints. In Philemon and Galatians the apostle says, "The grace of our Lord Jesus Christ be with your spirit." It is only meant for spiritual-minded men, for such as have been born again of the Holy Spirit. In I Cor. 16:21-24 he pronounces a solemn curse upon those whom he feels he cannot bless, because they are so base as not to love the infinitely loving Jesus.

III. What will be the Result if this Grace Be With You All? Blessed consequences will accrue to —

A. Yourselves.

1. You will love God better.

2. You will be much in prayer, for this eminently distinguished his character.

3. You will walk with God, even as he did.

B. Your fellow Church-members.

1. You will love each other with a pure heart fervently.

2. Your speech will be to edification.

C. Your families. The servants will find the house a home, and the children will become children of God, when the master and mistress are filled with the grace of our Lord Jesus.

D. The world.   — Charles H. Spurgeon

72. The Great Argument for Abstinence
(I Cor. 8:11-13)

I. Arguments for Abstinence Are Often Grounded On —

A. Danger to ourselves.

1. We may be led to excess.

2. We may injure ourselves, physically or morally.

B. Wastefulness.

C. Intrinsical wrongness.

II. Such Arguments Frequently Lack Cogency.

A. The third will have no application to a large class of things indifferent in themselves, and it is generally in respect of such that the war is waged.

B. The others are open to question. Conflicting facts will be adduced, and where knowledge is imperfect the contest is likely to continue. And the argument often acts as a temptation, for when human nature is warned of peril it often delights to show how brave and steadfast it can be.

III. The Apostolic Argument. St. Paul —

A. Enlarge the view so that others are included as well as ourselves. Abstinence is sometimes not for ourselves at all, but only for our fellows (Phil. 2:4). We are units, but united units. We cannot legislate for that little area which we ourselves occupy.

B. Recognizes the influence of example. Our words are a spider's web; our acts are a cable. Men do what we show them, not what we tell them. And we cannot persuade men that we are strong and they weak.

C. Asserts the obligation of self-sacrifice for the welfare of others. That which is "indifferent" becomes anything but that if our indulgence is injurious to others. Our sacrifice is small indeed compared with their possible loss. This argument has special force for Christians.

1. They have the example of self-sacrifice in their Master (v. 12). They have a more impressive view of the issues involved in the fall of a fellow-creature.

2. Their non-abstinence may be a sin against a fellow-Christian (v. 11). The fall may be, not of an unbeliever, but of a brother associated in Christian fellowship and service, and thus be —

3. A sin against the brethren (v. 12), i.e., the Church, bringing scandal and disgrace through a brother's fall. And also —

4. A sin against Christ (v. 12). For Christ and Christians are one — He the Head and they the members.

5. They have in their ears such utterances of their Master's as Matt. 18:6; 25:40.   — W. E. HURNDALL

73. Charity (I Cor. 13:1-13)

Each of the apostles had a predominant feature of character. Paul's was faith; John's love. And yet it was not to John that the office was assigned of expounding his own especial grace. The reason for this is, if Paul had exalted faith only, and John love only, we might have conceived that the judgment of each was guided by his pecularities of temperament. But when the gifted apostle counts gifts as nothing in comparison of love, no doubt remains.

I. THE DESCRIPTION OF THIS GRACE (v. 4-7).

A. This is needed, because no single word can express its fulness. Many of these qualities are what we should assign to other graces, e.g., patience, "suffereth long"; generosity, "envieth not"; humility, "vaunteth not herself"; dignified demeanor, "doth not behave itself unseemly," etc. But it is in the co-existence of all that the real life of the under-root of love was shown.

B. The apostle here describes a Christian gentleman. The difference between high-breeding or courtesy, i.e., manners of the court, the characteristic of the high-born, and Christian courtesy is, that the former gracefully insists upon its own rights; the latter gracefully remembers the rights of others. The Spirit of Christ does really what high-breeding only does outwardly. A high-bred man is urbane even to persons whom he is inwardly cursing; and hence the only true deep refinement comes from Christian love. And hence, too, we understand what is meant by elevating and refining the poorer classes. Christianity desires to make them all gentlemen. Only read this description of Christian charity, and conceive it existing in a peasant's breast. Could he be rude, selfish, and inconsiderate? Would he not be a gentleman in heart?

II. THE REASONS FOR ITS SUPERIORITY TO GIFTS.

A. Its permanence — "Charity never faileth."

1. Prophecy — the power of interpreting Scripture, is a precious gift, but a time will come "when they shall not teach every man his neighbor, saying, Know the Lord, but all shall know Him from the least to the greatest."

2. Tongues also shall pass away. Suppose a man had known fifty languages in the days of St. Paul, how few would be of use now!

3. Knowledge also "shall vanish away," for it is but a temporary state of the human mind, e.g.,

a. That of the physician, which arises out of the existence of disease: were there no disease, his knowledge would disappear.

b. It is the same with gifts of healing; when the time comes in which "they shall hunger no more, and thirst no more," when sickness and death shall cease, this power shall be needless.

c. So also with the knowledge of the lawyer. Were there no wrongs done, the necessity of legal knowledge would be at an end.

d. The same with science, which is ever shifting and becoming obsolete. The science of St. Paul's day is only curious now.

B. Its completeness. Gifts are only means to an end. Love remains, the perfection of our human being, just as stem, flower, bud, and leaf in the tree are all subservient to the fruit. St. Paul uses two illustrations to make this plain (v. 11, 12).

1. Just what childhood is to manhood, the most advanced manhood is to our heavenly being. There are many things now which subserve a high purpose, but do not belong to the highest state.

Patriotism, ambition, exclusive friendship, will then disappear, and be succeeded by higher impulses.

2. Just what the going out of a room lighted through frosted glass into the clear daylight would be to us now, will be the entrance of the purified spirit unto God's realities out of this world of shadows — of things half seen — of restless dreams (I John 3:2).   — FREDERICK W. ROBERTSON

74. Spiritul Warfare (II Cor. 10:4)

I. THE WARFARE.

A. A moral warfare. It is the case of truth against error; of knowledge against ignorance and superstition; of liberty against vassalage; of holiness against sin. Its object is that the kingdom of darkness may be overthrown and the kingdom of Christ established.

B. A necessary contest. It is not optional. We must conquer or be conquered.

C. An arduous conflict. It cannot be maintained by an idle show on the parade, but only by actual and persevering service.

1. Our enemies are numerous. We wrestle not against flesh and blood.

2. Our enemies are ever on the alert. We cannot with safety reckon on any cessation of hostilities.

D. A most momentous struggle. In it are involved interests the most solemn and interminable.

II. THE WEAPONS.

A. Every Christian is a soldier, and he puts on the whole armor of God (Eph. 6:11, etc.). Those engaged in this warfare fight according to prescribed laws. Wherever they go they erect the standard of the King of kings. They fight and conquer by their faithful preaching, holy living, works of faith, and labors of love.

B. These weapons are not carnal. Men are not to be dragooned into Christianity. Errors are not to be cut to pieces by the sword.

C. But though they are not carnal, they are real and powerful.

1. Compared with those used by the warriors of this world! What can they do? — they can wound the body; but the soul

defies their power. But here are weapons which can take hearts prisoners, and carry them away in delightful captivity.

2. Compared with the weapons of those who oppose themselves to Christ — the jests of impiety — the subtleties of sophistry, the feathered arrows of sarcasm. When by the means of these has ever error been wrung from the heart?

D. Whence arises this might? Let us take care not to attribute too much to our weapons. They are mighty through God. He furnishes and accompanies the right use of them with His presence and power.

III. THE ISSUE.

A. The pulling down of strongholds. The enemy, after having been worsted in open conflict, flees to the strongholds; but we are to lay siege to and destroy the foe in their very fortresses. And what is any unregenerate heart but a stronghold? Men are under the influence of the spirit that worketh in the hearts of the children of disobedience. Is he not fortified there by ignorance, by pride, by corrupt passions, by unbelief?

B. "Casting down imaginations, and every high thing," etc. The allusion here is to those machines which were employed to destroy walls and towers of defense. The terms apply equally well to "philosophy, falsely so called." How many high things are there still in the world which must be cast down!

C. The captivity of every thought to the obedience of Christ.

1. The enemy has been pursued, his fortresses have been thrown down, his citadel has been taken, and every individual within has been carried away in triumph. The whole man with all his powers is overcome. This is a victory such as the warriors of this world never achieved. Bodies may be taken captive, still the thoughts are free. But here is a conquest over the thoughts.

2. And this captivity is as honorable and delightful as it is complete. What can be more degrading than to be a captive of sin and Satan? — but to be taken captive by Christ, and to be obedient to Him — What an honor, What a joy!

Conclusion: We may learn that our common Christianity —

1. Is not a system of seclusion and quietism. It is a warfare. Neutrality is out of the question here. "Curse ye Meroz," etc.

2. Is not only defensive, but aggressive. The principal reason why the gospel has not made more progress in the world is this: we have contented ourselves with a defensive rather than an

aggressive warfare. What are we doing — defending the outworks, showing our dexterity in distinguishing nice points, and sometimes wounding a fellow-soldier, perhaps, because his uniform differs from our own? This we have done, instead of uniting in one broad phalanx against the common foe!

3. Is destined ultimately to triumph.

— Richard Newton

75. Remembrance of the Poor Recommended
(Gal. 2:10)

I. The Nature of the Assertion.

A. Remember the Work of the Poor.

1. Their work is irksome and laborious.

2. Their work is often detrimental to health.

3. But their work is chiefly beneficial.

B. Remember the deprivations of the poor.

C. The remembrance of the poor should be founded on a personal acquaintance with their circumstances.

II. The Obligation We Are Under to Comply with It.

A. The dictates of humanity require it.

B. The demands of duty require it.

C. The rights of justice require it.

D. The claims of interest require it.

III. Objections Answered.

A. "My circumstances are such that I have nothing to spare." Think of the poor widow and the mites.

B. "Charity must begin at home." But remember, it must not *end* at home.

C. "I have a right to do what I will with my own." But what is your own? Are you not a steward?

C. "The poor do not deserve to be remembered." But their merit is not the ground for our benevolence. We are to "be merciful, as our Father in heaven is merciful." — Charles Simeon

76. The Sword (Eph. 6:17)

I. THE SWORD IS RECOMMENDED. Observe —

A. The sword itself. Is "the Word of God."

B. The description given of this sword — "Sword of the Spirit."

1. It is the production of the Spirit — "All Scripture is given by inspiration of God" (II Tim. 3:16). (See also II Peter 1:19-21.)

2. It is the instrument which the Holy Spirit makes use of in effecting His purposes.

3. It is by the Spirit's influence believers can profitably use the Word of God.

II. WHEN THE SWORD OF THE SPIRIT MAY BE EMPLOYED.

A. Satan's assaults are to be resisted by it.

B. The world's attacks are to be overcome by it.

C. When our own hearts would deceive us.

1. By distrust and despondency.

2. When in danger of self-complacency.

3. When inclined to indolence.

III. SOME DIRECTIONS FOR EFFECTUALLY WIELDING IT.

A. Cultivate an intimate acquaintance with it.

B. Keep this sword polished and bright. This is only to be done by constant exercise.

C. Seek, by constant prayer, a renewal of spiritual strength.

Application:

1. Learn from this not to wage war with unhallowed weapons; such as human reason — such as human passion.

2. The weapon provided is all-sufficient.

3. Use it for all spiritual purposes.

— JABEZ BURNS

77. Love Abounding Through Knowledge (Phil. 1:9)

This climax is unexpected. We should have thought "in fervor, zeal, self-sacrifice." Instead of that the direction is upward from the heart to the head.

I. Knowledge Reveals Character and Character Draws out Love. We can only love a person whom we know to be lovable. This holds especially true of our relations to God. Enmity comes of ignorance of Him. Hence, in Jesus He has given us a revelation of His heart, and to know Christ is to love God. "My people is destroyed for lack of knowledge," is the epitaph written over the graves of scores of dead Christians. Neglecting the diligent study of the Scriptures they have no nutriment for their love, and it starves.

II. Knowledge of God Brings Us Into Communion with that Divine Life Which Is the Spring of All Divine Love. If God is love, the more we come into fellowship with Himself the more we shall come into the exercise and experience of His love. But it is only through knowledge that we can come into this experience. — Adoniram J. Gordon

78. The Christian Life (Col. 2:6, 7)

I. The Great Blessing. "Ye have received Christ Jesus the Lord."

A. Acceptance of Christ. A voluntary act.

B. Possession of Christ. Having received Him He is ours, and we share all His acts.

1. Christ died: we die with Him (Gal. 2:20), and so are free from the penalty of sin in the eyes of the law.

2. Christ was buried (v. 12) and we with Him, and so became dead to our former life (Rom. 6:4).

3. Christ rose, and we rise with Him into newness of life (v. 13).

4. Christ is at the right hand of God, and we ascend with Him into the honors, and safety of the heavenly life (chap. 3:1-3).

II. The Urgent Duty.

A. Walk, implying —

1. Progress, not only motion. There may be motion in the sap of a plant, but the plant is fixed; and in a ball struck by a bat, but that is forced, not voluntary; but a walk implies personal activity. So in the Christian walk.

a. We must not stay at the starting-point.

b. We must not loiter, "Forgetting the things behind."

c. We must not walk as in a circle, "laying agin the foundation of repentance," etc.

2. Change of scene. In a walk our eyes are ever dwelling on something fresh. So we must ever be finding something new in Christ.

3. Our walk is to be "in Him." He is to be seen in us. Others are to know our Master by our life.

B. Rooted in Him.

1. The root gives stability to the tree. Those trees are most stable whose roots take the largest and deepest hold.

2. The life of a tree depends upon its rootedness; uproot it and you destroy it. So we die if not rooted in Christ our Life.

C. Built up in Him.

1. Constant additions.

2. Growing solidity.

3. Ultimate perfection.

4. Exhibition of the Architect's skill, patience, and power.

D. Stablished in the faith. We must have Christ in us or we shall be overthrown. We are not to be a vane turning at every breath of wind, nor a plant taking such slight hold that some stronger blast will overthrow; but like an oak or a house on a rock, so stablished that no power can move. This is necessary in view of the various influences to which Christian life is exposed.

III. The Strong Motive.

A. The obligation — "As." Having received Christ we are bound to walk in Him.

B. The appeal — "Ye." Think of what you were and what Christ has made you. Show your gratitude by walking in Him.

— John Gill

79. Christ Our Life (Col. 3:4)

What is meant by *life?* The word is very comprehensive, and includes —

A. Appropriate activity.

B. Happiness. The life here intended is

1. Not natural life;

2. Not intellectual life;

3. But, spiritual and eternal life.

Christ is our life in that He is —

I. ITS AUTHOR.

A. He saves us from death.

1. By His atonement which satisfies the law.

2. By delivering us from the power of Satan.

B. He is the author of inward spiritual life. Because —

1. He procures for us the gift of the life-giving Spirit. He has redeemed us in order that He might receive the promise of the Spirit.

2. He not only merits, but imparts the gift of the Holy Spirit.

II. ITS OBJECT.

A. The exercises in which Christian life consists terminate in Him.

B. The happiness involved consists in fellowship with Him. He is our life as He is our joy, portion, inheritance.

III. ITS END. It is Christ for us to live. While others live for themselves — some for their country, some for mankind — the believer lives for Christ. It is the great design of his life to promote Christ's glory and advance His kingdom.

Inferences:

1. Test of character. The difference between the true and nominal Christian lies here. The one seeks and regards Christ as His life only as He delivers from death; the other as the end and object of life.

2. The true way to grow in grace, or to get life, is to come to Christ.

3. The happiness and duty of thus making Christ our life.

— CHARLES HODGE

80. The Habitual Recognition of God (I Thess. 1:3, 4)

I. WHAT IT IS TO ACT AS EVER IN THE SIGHT OF GOD. To maintain a supreme and habitual regard for God in the relations He sustains towards us.

A. Some act with a perpetual self-consciousness. They care for no one's esteem or condemnation. Their one object is to please self — a poor master when best pleased.

B. Some act with a perpetual consciousness of others: ever fearful to offend, and offending from very fearfulness; ever overanxious to please, and failing through very overanxiousness.

C. The Christian is ever conscious of, "Thou God seest me."

1. As a Being of infinite perfection.

2. As Lawgiver and Sovereign.

3. As Creator, Preserver, Benefactor.

4. As Redeemer and Sanctifier.

5. As Judge and Rewarder.

6. As Father.

II. THE ADVANTAGE OF ACTING AS EVER IN THE SIGHT OF GOD.

A. It would make the whole of life a continued act of religion. Apply this to business, politics, domestic duties.

B. It would give us the comfort of knowing that someone whose appreciation is worth having is cognizant of little acts upon which men set no value. Who regards the widow's mite or the cup of cold water? God is also observant of those little trials in the factory or home, the aggregate of which constitute a great trial. He is looking down with sympathy — be brave; He is looking down with justice — beware.

C. It would strengthen against temptation. There is enough in that omniscient Being to gratify every longing. Why, then, try to fill your belly with the husks that the swine do eat?

D. It would make us stedfast in all holy obedience. We should be prepared for all the duties of devotion. The sense of God with us amid all the cares and bustle of the world would help to maintain all the graces in lively exercise.

E. It would prepare for death and eternity.

— NATHANIEL W. TAYLOR

81. Rejoice Evermore (I Thess. 5:16-18)

I. WHAT IS IT TO REJOICE? There is —

A. A joy in outward things.

1. Natural.

2. Sinful (Eccl. 11:9).

3. Lawful (Eccl. 2:24; 3:12, 13, 22).

B. A spiritual joy in God (Phil. 3:1; 4:4).

II. What Is It To Rejoice Always in the Lord? To make Him the object of all our joy.

A. For what He is in Himself (Matt. 19:17).

B. For what He is to us.

1. Our Preserver (Ps. 46:1, 2).

2. Our Saviour (Hab. 3:18; Ps. 27:1).

3. Our God (Heb. 8:10).

III. Why Ought We to Rejoice Evermore?

A. God commands it (Ps. 32:11; Phil. 4:4).

B. Christ prays for it (John 17:13).

C. The Holy Ghost works it (John 14:26; 17:7).

D. It is necessary and useful.

1. To lessen our esteem of the world and of sinful pleasures. (Ps. 4:7; 84:10).

2. To enlarge our hearts and make them more capacious of heavenly things.

3. To facilitate our duties, and make us active in God's service (Deut. 28:47; Neh. 8:10).

4. To support us under our troubles (I Peter 1:7, 8).

IV. How We May Always Rejoice?

A. Live above the world (II Cor. 4:18).

B. Live above the natural temper of your bodies.

C. Avoid such things as are apt to grieve and trouble you.

1. Sin (Ps. 51:8; Matt. 26:75; II Cor. 1:12).

2. Needless questions —

a. About God's decrees.

b. The exact time of your conversion.

c. Judging yourselves according to your outward condition (Eccl. 9:1).

D. Whatsoever happens still put your trust in God (Isa. 49:13, 14; 1:10; 55:7; Heb. 13:6).

E. Act your faith constantly in Christ (John 14:1; Rom. 8:33, 34).

F. Often meditate on the happiness of those who truly fear God.

1. In the world (Rom. 8:28).

2. In the world to come (I Cor. 2:9).

G. Check thyself whensoever thou findest thy spirits begin to sink (Ps. 42:5, 11).

— WILLIAM BEVERIDGE

82. The Coming of Christ (II Thess. 2:1)

I. THE NATURE OF IT. Christ came. He comes. He is to come.

A. He came in the flesh. The long line of predictions from Adam to Malachi were accomplished at last, after long delay and anxious expectation.

B. He comes continually.

1. In the extraordinary manifestation of His presence and power, whether for judgment or mercy.

2. In the special manifestation of Himself to His people.

C. He is to come.

1. Personally and visibly.

2. With power and great glory.

3. The dead shall rise, the just and the unjust.

4. The judgment will then be held.

5. The world destroyed.

6. The kingdom of God consummated. The consequences to His people will be —

a. Their redemption, i.e. their final deliverance from the power of death.

b. Their complete conformity to the likeness of Christ.

c. Their perfect enjoyment of that kingdom prepared for them from the foundation of the world.

II. THE TIME.

A. It is unrevealed.

B. It is to be unexpected.

C. It will not be until the conversion of the Jews and the calling in of the Gentiles. Did the apostles expect Christ in their day?

1. They regarded His coming as they regarded the coming of death.

2. It was revealed to them there should be a falling away first. We must distinguish between their personal expectations and their teaching. The latter alone is infallible.

III. Points of Analogy Between the First and Second Comings.

A. Both predicted.

B. Anxiously and long expected.

C. The subjects of much speculation as to time and mode.

D. Disappointing in the one and the other.

IV. The State of Mind Which the Doctrine Should Induce.

A. A firm belief in the revealed fact that He is to come. This faith should not be shaken by long delay. How long Abraham waited and died without the sight!

B. Earnest desire. The hopes of the ancient people were concentrated on the coming of the Messiah. This led them to bear patiently what they had to suffer. To set their hopes on the future and not on the present. The same effect should be produced on us.

C. Watchfulness and anxiety, lest that day should overtake us as a thief in the night. We should have our lamps trimmed and our lights burning. It would be a dreadful thing for Christ to come and find us immersed in the world.

D. Prayer and waiting.

E. Solicitous efforts to prepare others for His coming, and to prepare the way of the Lord. He will not come to the individual nor to the Church till His way is prepared.
This includes —

1. Taking out of the way obstructions to His coming.

2. The accomplishment of the ingathering of His people.

— Charles Hodge

83. Seen of Angels (I Tim. 3:16)

I. Explaining This Subject.

A. Angels were witnesses of the most important events which concerned the Redeemer.

B. The angels, who beheld this amazing scene, were honored to minister to Jesus in these His sufferings. Thus, after our Lord's temptation in the wilderness, we read, "Then the devil leaveth Him, and behold angels come and minister unto Him" (Matt. 4: 11).

C. Angels behold and pry into the grand designs, for which Infinite Wisdom ordained all this scene of condescension and suffering. They not only saw God manifest in the flesh, but they saw the purposes for which He was thus manifest, for which He lived, for which He died.

D. While beholding the love which prompted the Son of God thus to condescend and thus to suffer, angels learn to love, and willingly to attend upon, and minister to the meanest of those whom the Lord of angels loved, and for whose salvation He stooped so low.

E. Angels, who saw God manifest in the flesh, were the first publishers to man of some of the most important events which they witnessed. An angel acquainted Daniel that the Messiah should be cut off, though not for Himself. An angel was the first publisher of the Saviour's birth.

II. A FEW PRACTICAL REFLECTIONS.

A. How shocking the folly and ingratitude of many! Angels desire to look into the mysteries of grace: and men, more nearly concerned in them, esteem it a disparagement to bestow upon them one serious thought. They shut their eyes, despise and scoff, while angels gaze, and wonder, and adore.

B. Imitate angels. The sufferings and glory of the Redeemer are their favorite meditation. Let them also be yours. Count all things loss and dung for the excellency of the knowledge of Christ.

C. Rejoice that He who was seen of angels was manifest in the flesh. Triumph, oh Christian, in that name Immanuel, God with us. In creation man was made a little lower than angels. In redemption, the Son of God, by assuming our nature, has done infinitely greater honor to us than to them.

D. Ask you hearts, Have we ever seen the Lord? You have heard of Him with the hearing of the ear. Have you, by the eye of faith, so seen Him as to abhor yourselves, and repent in dust and ashes? Doth beholding His glory remove prejudice against Him, captivate your hearts and transform you to His image?

— JOHN ERSKINE

84. Lovers of Pleasure Described and Warned
(II Tim. 3:2-5)

I. WHO BELONG TO THIS NUMBER?

A. All whose fondness for pleasure leads them to violate the commands of God.

1. By indulging in forbidden pleasures.

2. By inordinate pursuit of pleasures not in themselves sinful or expressly forbidden.

B. All who are led by a fondness for pleasure to indulge in amusements which they suspect may be wrong, or which they do not feel crtain are right. When we love any person supremely, we are careful to avoid not only those things which we know will displease him, but such as we suspect may do it.

C. All who find more satisfaction in the pursuit of wordly pleasures than they do in God's service.

D. All who are deterred from immediately embracing the Savior, and commencing a religious life, by an unwillingness to renounce the pleasures of the world, are most certainly lovers of pleasures more than lovers of God.

II. THEIR SINFUL, GUILTY, AND DANGEROUS CONDITION.

A. That the apostle considered them as sinful, in no common degree, is evident from the company in which he has placed them. It is still further evident from the description which he gives of them in some of the verses succeeding the text. For instance, he there informs us that such are persons of corrupt minds. What to his Creator, can be a more satisfactory proof of a corrupt state of mind in a rational, immortal being, than a preference of unsatisfying, transitory, sinful pleasures.

B. In the second place the apostle informs us that they resist the truth. This they must do, for their deeds are evil. Such persons hate the truth, because the truth condemns their sinful but beloved pleasures.

C. Hence they are represented as despisers of good men. They consider such men, whose conduct reproves them, as the enemies of their happiness, and ridicule them as rigid, morose, superstitious, or hypocritical persons, and who will neither enjoy the world themselves, nor allow others to do it.

D. Lastly, the persons we are describing are represented as being dead in trespasses and sins. He that liveth in pleasure, is dead while he lives. They are dead as it respects the great end of their existence; dead to everything that is good; dead in the sight of a holy God; loathsome to Him as a corpse is to us, and as unfit for the society of the living Jehovah, as the naturally dead are for the society of the living.   — EDWARD PAYSON

85. The Holy War (II Tim. 4:6-8)

I.   THE TWO ARMIES.

A. The army of the saints.

1. Their Captain-General is the Lord Jesus Christ.

2. The officers are the ministers of Christ, and all who are active and useful in His service.

3. The soldiers are the saints.

4. The enlisting — conversion.

5. The uniform — the graces of the Spirit, and the robe of righteousness.

6. The armor — helmet of salvation, etc.

7. The instruction of the young soldiers — Bible.

8. The allies — angels.

B. The army of the enemy.

1. Generals — sin, Satan, and world.

2. Soldiers — the wicked.

3. Allies — evil spirits.

II.   THE BATTLE.

A. What kind of a battle?

1. A good battle.

2. A hot battle.

3. A very profitable battle.

4. A battle that must be constant.

B. Where fought? Whole world.

C. When shall it be finished? At death for each individual soldier; at the day of judgment for the whole army.

III.   THE VICTORY.

A. Is certain.

B. Shall be held in everlasting remembrance,

— A. FLETCHER

86. Sober-Mindedness (Titus 2:6)

I. YOUNG MEN NEED THIS PARTICULAR COUNSEL.

A. They are inexperienced as to the world.

B. They are but little acquainted with their own hearts.

C. They are surrounded on every side with evil counsellors and bad examples.

II. COUNSEL WHICH THIS PARTICULAR SITUTATION REQUIRES.

A. General.

1. Imbue your soul deeply with the concerns of eternity.

2. Pray God to guide you every step of the way.

3. Be diligent in the study of the word of God.

B. Particular

1. Consider what becomes you in your particular place and station.

2. Consider on every occasion what impression your conduct is likely to make on others.

3. Choose for your associates the prudent and discreet.

4. Examine your own motives and principles of action, with all possible care and diligence.

5. Be open to convictions.   — CHARLES SIMEON

87. Praises and Prayers (Philem. 4)

I. THE OBJECT. "I thank my *God*."

A. God is the Author of all good (Hos. 14:8).

B. To him, therefore, is all praise due (I Chron. 29:13, 14).

C. It is the privilege of all his children to approach him as their God.

D. Our prayers and praises should be for others as well as for ourselves.

II. THE CIRCUMSTANCE. *"Always."*

III. THE MATTER.

A. *Praises* on account of Philemon.

1. Love for Christ.

2. Faith in Christ.

3. Love to the Saints.

B. *Prayer* to God.

1. That fruits may abound.

2. That others may be won.

3. That God may be glorified.

— MATTHEW HENRY

88. Saints Pilgrims on Earth (Heb. 11:11, 12)

I. WHAT IS INCLUDED IN THE METAPHOR.

A. The pilgrim's original home was in the city of destruction.

B. His pilgrimage commenced through the influence of the gospel on his heart.

C. By faith in God's testimony he set his face towards the heavenly Zion.

D. As a pilgrim he claims no possession in the country through which he passes.

E. As a pilgrim he travels onwards towards the city of habitation.

II. THE QUALIFICATIONS AND DUTIES INVOLVED IN IT.

A. A pilgrim's heart. And that is a renewed heart; one delivered from the love of sin and the world.

B. A pilgrim's head. A knowledge of his way; of the good old way; the way revealed in the Holy Scriptures; a way written in the luminous words of God; a way trodden by all preceding pilgrims journeying to Zion.

C. A pilgrim's spirit. The spirit which has animated every child of God.

1. Of devotion and direct intercourse with God.

2. Of praise; singing His statutes, and rejoicing in His grace.

3. Of self-denial: sacrificing self, and submitting fully to the will of God.

4. Of faith and hope: believing and trusting in the truth and goodness of the promises of God.

5. Of vigilance, to watch against enemies and perils.

6. Of perseverance: holding on his way.

D. A pilgrim's resources.

1. His staff on which to lean. And this is the pledged promise of God, that His own presence shall go with him, and never, never leave him.

2. His provisions: bread and water given him from heaven. The true manna and the streams of salvation. "If any man thirst."

3. His houses of entertainment. Places where he can be welcomed to the hospitable board and chamber of repose. These are the ordinances of religion, and the various social and private means of grace.

4. Suitable raiment, and especially sandals for his journey. "Thy shoes shall be iron and brass . . ." "Feet shod . . ."

Application:

1. How really happy is the Christian pilgrim; his sorrows and crosses will soon be over, and that for ever: his present comforts and blessings are rich and numerous.

2. How glorious the end of his journey! The heavenly Jerusalem; the city of God; world of light, and life, and glory.

3. Urge sinners to set out on this spiritual pilgrimage.

— JABEZ BURNS

89. The Double-Minded Man Exposed (James 1:8)

It is a generally-acknowledged truth, that the mind constitutes the man. In human friendships, an insincere profession of regard will not stand a severe trial; but will fail us, when we most need a firm support. In religion too, if the heart be not right with God, we shall never persevere amidst the difficulties and dangers with which we shall be encompassed. That our faith will be tried, is certain; and that we shall need support from above, is certain: I may add too, that if we be "strong in faith, giving glory to God," we shall derive such aid from above, as shall carry us through all our temptations, how great soever they may be, and make us "more than conquerors" over all our enemies. But, if we are of a doubtful mind, we shall never finally maintain our steadfastness; but shall draw back when dangers threaten us, and faint when trials come upon us; for "the double-minded man is unstable in all his ways." Let us endeavor:

I. To ASCERTAIN THE CHARACTER HERE SPECIFIED. The Apostle is speaking solely respecting confidence in God: to that therfore we shall confine our observations. Were we to enter at large into the character of a "double-minded man," we should have a vast field before us, sufficient to occupy our attention through many discourses: but by adhering simply to the view proposed to us in the text, we shall best consult the scope of the Apostle's argument, and the edification of your minds.

"The double-minded man" then is one:

A. Whose reliance on God is not simple.

B. Whose confidence in God is not entire.

II. To Mark His Conduct — "He is unstable in all his ways," and is ever liable to be turned from the truth.

A. In his principles.

B. In his practice.

Let us learn then from hence,

1. The vast importance of self-examination.

2. The indispensable necessity of being "renewed in the spirit of our minds."   — Charles Simeon

90. Christian Conversation (I Peter 2:12)

I. The Exhortation Implies at Least Three Things.

A. *Truth,* or veracity with respect to our words.

B. *Justice* and *equity* in our dealings, as well as *sincerity* and *truth* in all our conversation.

C. It includes *fidelity* with respect to our trust and engagements.

II. Motives by Which the Exhortation Is Enforced.

A. An upright and honest conversation would *stop the mouth of slanderers.*

B. It would *bring glory to God.*

— Charles Simeon

91. Preparation for the Second Coming of Christ
(II Peter 3:12)

I. One Effect of a True Love of Our Lord, Which Expects Him to Come to Judgment at the Last Great Day, Will be to Keep the Mind and Heart of Man Free From

DISTRACTING FORMS OF EXCITEMENT. "The day of the Lord" has in all times been to men believing in Christ, but not loving Him, an occasion of disorderly walking, of idleness, and disobedience.

II. AND AGAIN, A TRUE LOVE OF OUR LORD IN VIEW OF HIS COMING AT THE DAY OF JUDGMENT IS GREATLY CONCERNED TO BE DOING THE BEST IT CAN WITH WHAT HE HAS GIVEN IN THE WAY OF ABILITY AND OF OPPORTUNITY.

III. ONE OTHER RESULT OF THE LOVE OF OUR LORD, OF WAITING FOR AND HASTING UNTO HIS COMING, WILL BE TO MAKE MUCH OF PRAYER, PRIVATE, AND PUBLIC, AS A PREPARATION FOR IT.

IV. IT MAY, INDEED, BE ASKED HOW, STRICTLY SPEAKING, WE CAN HASTEN TOWARD THE DAY OF GOD IN ANY OF THE WAYS DESCRIBED?

— CANON LIDDON

92. The Purifying Effect of Hope in Christ
(I John 3:3)

I. THE PRESENT PRIVILEGES AND FUTURE HOPE OF THE CHRISTIAN.

A. The present privilege of the Christian is to look up to God as his Father.

B. But this state of privilege is preparatory to something still higher, more precious and valuable.

II. IN WHOM AND ON WHAT BASIS IS HE PERMITTED TO ENTERTAIN SO GLORIOUS AND EXALTED A HOPE?

A. He has this hope in Christ Jesus our Lord; in God who hath given us His eternal Son to be the propitiation for our sins, and the Holy Spirit to them that obey Him.

B. His hope rests upon the work of Christ upon earth and His glorification in heaven.

III. THE EFFECT OF THE HOPE ON THE BELIEVER'S HEART AND LIFE.

A. This hope is calculated altogether to ensure his sanctification, to cleanse and sublimate his soul.

B. But what is the effect of hope in bringing about this purification? Much every way. The hope of the Christian is altogether calculated to elevate the soul and ennoble the character. Is he the inheritor of the kingdom of heaven, and shall he not prepare himself to take possession of his inheritance?

IV. But after What Model Must We Purify Ourselves? We must purify ourselves "even as He is pure." He must propose to himself no faulty or defective pattern. — H. J. Hastings

93. A Christian Family (II John 4)

I. A Christian Mother.
A. A Praying Mother.
B. An Exemplary Mother.
C. A Watchful Mother.
D. A Happy Mother.
II. The Children.
A. They Believed the Truth — i.e., they were converted.
B. They Loved the Truth.
C. They Lived the Truth.
III. The Religious Education of Children Is a Duty.

94. Soul Health (III John 2)

I. We Will Examine the Words of the Text.
A. "I wish"; more correctly, "I pray." Prayer is a wish sanctified. Turn your wishes into prayers.
B. "That thou mayest prosper." We may ask for prosperity for our friends; especially if, like Gaius, they serve God and His cause with their substance.
C. "And be in health." This is necessary to the enjoyment of prosperity. What would all else be without it?
D. "Even as thy soul prospereth." We are startled at this wish: the spiritual health of Gaius is made the standard of his outward properity! Dare we pray thus for many of our friends? Dare we pray thus for ourselves? What would be the result if such a prayer were answered?

II. WE WILL MENTION THE SYMPTOMS OF ILL-HEALTH.

A. A low temperature. Lukewarmness is an ill sign. In business, such a man will make but little way; in religion, none at all.

B. Contracted heart. If we do not love the brethren, there is something wrong with us.

C. A failing appetite as to spiritual food.

D. A difficulty in breathing. When prayer is an irksome duty, everything is wrong with us.

E. A general lethargy: unwillingness for holy service, want of heart, etc.

F. An ungovernable craving for unhealthy things.

III. WE WILL SUGGEST MEANS OF RECOVERY.

A. Seek good food. Study the Word.

B. Breathe freely. Do not restrain prayer.

C. Exercise yourself unto godliness. Labor for God.

D. Return to your native air: breathe the atmosphere of Calvary.

E. Live by the sea. Dwell near to God's all-sufficiency.

F. If these things fail, here is an old prescription: *"Carnis et Sanguinis Christi."* This taken several times a day, in a draught of the tears of repentance, is a sure cure.

IV. WE WILL CONCLUDE WITH AN EXHORTATION.

A. Brother Christian, is it a small matter to be weak and feeble? Thou needest all thy vigor. Go to Calvary, and recruit thyself.

B. Sinner, thou art dead, but life and health are in Christ!

— CHARLES H. SPURGEON

95. Church Disturbers (Jude 16)

I. INSINUATORS. The whisper, the shrug of the shoulder, the half sentence containing a surmise of the other half, and the warning of some awful revelation to some respecting the servant of God and his character, mark these men in every age. They succeed to create distrust of the ministry, and dry up the fountain of Christian sympathy and prayer.

II. FAULTFINDERS. Nothing is done to please them. They are on the alert to find out mistakes. They turn even the love feast into a scene of embitterment.

III. LIBERTINES. The root of their character is a love of sin —
some form of gross immorality. They hate the truth because it
exposes their villainy and shame.

IV. PRETENDERS. They are full of ostentation, fond of tall talk.
To the ignorant, loud swelling words sound grandly, but to the
wise, "the crackling of thorns under a pot."

V. DISSEMBLERS. They put on a smiling face, and speak
smooth words to persons of rank, to secure their approbation and
gain their support. They subject principles to appearances. Let
the mantle of Jude fall on our ministers.   — THOMAS W. DAVIES

96. The Spiritual Building (Jude 20)

I. BEFORE BUILDING.

A. Count the cost (Luke 14:28).

B. Prepare fit matter (II Chron. 2:8, 9; I Cor. 3:12).

C. Prepare skilful and faithful builders. Some build a wall,
but daub it with untempered mortar, which the shower and hail-
stones throw down again (Ezek. 13:11). Some flattering builders
there be that gild rotten posts and mud walls, and by flatteries
cause people to err (Jer. 23). Some that square their work by a
false rule; not the Word, but some profounder school-learning.

II. IN BUILDING.

A. Lay a good foundation, both for matter and manner.

1. The matter is Jesus Christ (I Cor. 3:11).

2. Then the manner of laying this foundation sure is to dig deep,
as you know the foundation of a great house had need to be. Lay
it in humility and godly sorrow, called in Heb. 6:1 the foundation
of repentance, because it can never be laid without a deep sense
of sorrow for sin, giving us a clear sight what need we have of
Christ.

B. The foundation thus laid. Lay all the materials skilfully
upon the same foundation; for building is an artificial coupling of
all materials by square upon the same foundation. So here —

1. There is use of many materials. In every mean house there
must be somewhat of everything, some stone, timber, lime, lead,
glass, iron, and in this building must be some degrees of all graces
— some faith, hope, love, knowledge, and the rest. Faith as gates

of brass, and door to let us in unto Christ and His Church for salvation; knowledge as windows to lighten the house, or else all would be dark; hope as the glass or casements to look out unto things believed, specially the life to come; love as the cement to knit all together; patience as the pillars, bearing all the weight of the house, etc.

2. These and the rest of the graces must be laid together (1I Peter 1:5).

3. By line and square of the Word (Exod. 25:40).

4. All upon the same foundation — Christ.

C. Build up to the laying of the roof and ridge tiles, still striving to perfection (Heb. 6:1; Eph. 2:21).

III.   AFTER BUILDING.

A. As the Jews, having built an house, must dedicate it to the Lord, so do thou. Especially the temple and tabernacle were solemnly set apart for His service and sacrifices. Do thou also offer in this house the daily sacrifice of prayer, praise, alms which smell sweet (Phil. 4:18). Let it be the house of prayer, a spiritual house, to offer spiritual sacrifices, acceptable to God by Jesus Christ (I Peter 2:5). Yea, offer thy soul and body a reasonable sacrifice, living and holy (Rom. 12:1), which is the right dedication of thy house.

B. Furnish thy house with needful utensils.

— T. TAYLOR

97. Divine Revelations (Rev. 1:1-3)

Christians are not confined to this world in their enjoyments of life. They behold not merely the things of men, but also the things of God; not merely the things of time, but also those of eternity.

I.   THEY PROCEED FROM THE INFINITE SOURCE OF KNOWLEDGE AND LOVE.

A. God is the primal author of spiritual revelations. He is the source of light, and alone can cause it to shine from heaven into the heart of man.

B. Christ is the sympathetic medium of spiritual revelations. John is here writing of Him as having ascended to heaven with a Divine-human nature.

C. Varied messengers are the communicating agencies of revelation. Angelic ministeries are interested in the instruction of the good. Who was the messenger here employed? It would seem that prophetic fires were kindled in some ancient seer who had entered upon his heavenly rest and that he was employed to uncover to the imprisoned apostle the sublime versions of this book.

II. THEY ARE GIVEN TO THOSE ENGAGED IN THE MORAL SERVICE OF THE UNIVERSE. "To show unto His servants."

A. They are not given to the nationally presumptuous. These have others visions more welcome to their ambitious spirits — visions of fame. They would rather dream of servile crowds paying them transient homage, than be permitted the grandest revelation of heaven that is possible to the human soul.

B. They are not given to the socially great. They are not given to kings by virtue of their kinghood. They are not given to the warrior in acknowledgment of his victory. They are not given to the wealthy in praise of their industry and thrift. They are rather given to the humble, to the poor in spirit, to the pure in heart, to the loving servants of the Lord.

C. They are not given to the intellectually wise. To untutored minds, but of heavenly thought, things divine are made known, far grander than are suspected by the students of earthly things. They are given to the good —

1. Because the good are in sympathy with God.

2. Because the good will live under the influence of the revelation.

3. Because the good will be faithful to the revelation.

III. THEY ARE GIVEN AT TIMES OF SOLITUDE AND GRIEF.

A. The good man's solitude is never lonely. But when earth is far removed, when the hurry of business and the excitement of pleasure are behind, then come those heavenly visions which so enrich the soul.

B. God does not forsake His faithful servants in their time of need. In the furnace we get bright visions of the Son of Man.

IV. THEY ARE DESIGNED TO INTERPRET THE EVENTFUL AGES OF MANKIND.

A. Man is unable to interpret the spiritual meaning of the ages.

B. The moral significance of the ages ought to engage our most careful study.

Lessons:

1. Adore the condescension of God in revealing Himself to man.

2. Praise the glory of God which He has manifested to your soul in time of vision.

3. Live and write the spiritual revelations of the Eternal.

— JOSEPH S. EXELL

98. The Philadelphian Conqueror (Rev. 3:12)

I. THE CONQUEROR IS TO BE A TEMPLE-PILLAR. Not an outside, but an inside pillar. The interior colonnades or double rows of tall pillars in some churches and temples are splendid beyond description. They are part of the vast fabric: not like those who minister there, going out and in, but standing immovable in their surpassing beauty. Such is the reward of the Philadelphian conqueror. An everlasting inhabitant and ornament of that sanctury of which we read, "I saw no temple therein . . ." They shall go no more out! Their home is the innermost shrine in the heavens. Like Jackin and Boaz (I Kings 1:15, 21), there they stand for ever.

II. THE CONQUEROR IS TO BE INSCRIBED WITH GLORIOUS NAMES. It is said of Christ that He has on His vesture and on His thigh a name written, "Kings of kings and Lord of lords." It is said of the redeemed in glory that they have their Father's name written on their foreheads (chap. 14:1); so here on these Philadelphian pillars are many names to be inscribed; each of them unutterably glorious. These inscriptions are written by Christ Himself: "I will write." He engraves these names upon these temple-pillars, that they may be eternal witnesses to them in the glorious sanctuary. The inscriptions to be thus engraven as follows:

A. "The name of my God." This is the name which God proclaimed to Moses, the name which is the summary of His blessed character, as the God of all graces. What honor! To be the marble on which Jehovah's name is carved, and from which it shall blaze forth in the eternal temple!

B. "The name of the city of my God." Other pillars set up on earth by man have the names of deities, or kings, or warriors, or cities graven upon them. But this inscription excels all in glory.

C. My "new name." This is the new name given by Christ, which no man knoweth save he who receivth it.

— HORATIUS BONAR

99. Christ's Kingly Authority (Rev. 19:11-16)

I. Christ, In His Mediatorial Character, Has a Crown of Supreme Dignity.

II. Christ, as Mediator, Has a Crown of Victory.

III. Jesus, as Mediator Has a Crown of Sovereign Power. Unto Him is given all power in heaven and upon earth: as far as the bounds of creation reach, so far does His dominion reach.

IV. Christ, as Mediator Has a Crown of Sovereign Right. He has not only the power to compel, but the right to demand the obedience of every creature; and it is the great distinction between those who are not His people, that while all the creatures of God, whether willingly or unwillingly, must execute Christ's pleasure, those who are indeed His submit joyfully and heartily to His rule, and keep themselves ready to do or suffer whatever He requires of them, simply because He requires it.

V. Jesus, as Mediator, Has a Crown of Judicial Authority: "The Father Himself judgeth no man, but hath committed all judgment to the Son," etc.   — Wm. Ramsay

100. The World Without a Sea (Rev. 21:1-8)

I. There Is No Division There. How much there is in this world that divides men! There are —

A. Social caste.

B. National prejudices.

C. Religious sectarianism.

D. Selfish interests.

E. Mutual misunderstandings. None of these will exist in heaven.

II. There Is No Mutation There. The only change is that of progress.

A. Progress in higher intelligence.

B. In loftier services.

C. In nobler fellowship. No change in the way of loss. The crown, the kingdom, the inheritance — all imperishable.